# Salinas River National Wildlife Refuge
## *Comprehensive Conservation Plan*

Prepared by:
U.S. Fish and Wildlife Service
Region 1

California/Nevada Refuge Planning Office
2800 Cottage Way, W-1916
Sacramento, CA 95825

San Francisco Bay National Wildlife Refuge Complex
1 Marshlands Road
Newark, CA 94536

Approved: _P. Kenneth McDermond_       Date: DEC 2 0 2002
Acting California Nevada Operations Manager

Implementation of this Comprehensive Conservation Plan and alternative management actions/programs have been assessed consistent with the requirements of the National Environmental Policy Act (42 USC 4321 et seq.).

# *Table of Contents*

# *Appendices*

# Figures

# Tables

# Chapter 1. Introduction and Background

## Content and Purpose of This Document

This document is a Comprehensive Conservation Plan (CCP) designed to guide the management of the Salinas River National Wildlife Refuge in Monterey County, California for the next 15 years. The U.S. Fish and Wildlife Service's (Service) management planning process for National Wildlife Refuges (NWRs) involves two phases: (1) the development of a broad Comprehensive Conservation Plan (CCP) that articulates a vision and specific goals for the refuge, and (2) the formulation of more detailed "step-down" management plans that enable the implementation of the CCP's vision.

The purposes of this CCP are:

- To provide a clear statement of direction for the management of the Salinas River National Wildlife Refuge (Refuge) over the next 15 years;
- To provide long-term continuity in Refuge management;
- To communicate the Service's management priorities for the Salinas River NWR to its neighbors and visitors and to the public;
- To provide an opportunity for the public to help shape the future management of the Salinas River NWR;
- To ensure that management programs on the Salinas River NWR are consistent with the mandates of the National Wildlife Refuge System (Refuge System) and the purpose of the Refuge as stated in establishing legislation;
- To ensure that the management of the Salinas River NWR is consistent with Federal, State, and local plans; and
- To provide a basis for budget requests to support the Salinas River NWR's needs for staffing, operations, maintenance, and capital improvements.

**Sand verbena (*Verbena* sp.)**
*USFWS Photo*

This document incorporates a CCP and three new step-down plans: an Avian Predator Management Plan, Wildland Fire Management Plan, and Hunt Plan. In addition, the existing Predator Management Plan (U.S. Fish and Wildlife Service 1993a) will remain in place as a step-down plan.

When it is implemented, this CCP will further the purposes and goals of the Salinas River National Wildlife Refuge, contribute to the overall mission of the National Wildlife Refuge System (see page 3), and address other relevant mandates, such as recovery of endangered species.

Chapter 2 describes the CCP planning process. Chapter 3 presents the management program proposed in this CCP.

## Need for This CCP

The National Wildlife Refuge System Improvement Act of 1997 (Public Law 105-57) (Improvement Act) requires that all Federal refuges be managed in accordance with an approved CCP by 2012. Moreover, the Salinas River National Wildlife Refuge currently has no integrated plan that guides the management of all of its resources and uses. In order to meet the dual needs of complying with the Improvement Act and providing long-term integrated management guidance for the Refuge, the Service proposes this CCP.

## The U.S. Fish and Wildlife Service and the National Wildlife Refuge System

### *U.S. Fish and Wildlife Service Responsibilities*

The Service is the primary Federal agency responsible for conserving and enhancing the Nation's fish and wildlife populations and their habitats. Although the Service shares this responsibility with other Federal, State, Tribal, local, and private entities, the Service has specific responsibilities for migratory birds, threatened and endangered species, anadromous fish, and certain marine mammals. The Service has similar responsibilities for the lands and waters it administers to support the conservation and enhancement of fish and wildlife.

### *The National Wildlife Refuge System*

The National Wildlife Refuge System is the world's largest collection of lands specifically managed for fish and wildlife conservation. Operated and managed by the Service, it comprises more than 500 national wildlife refuges with a combined area of more than 92 million acres. The majority of refuge lands (approximately 77 million acres) are located in Alaska. The remaining 15 million acres are spread across the other 49 states and several island territories.

National Wildlife Refuge System Mission and Goals. The mission of the National Wildlife Refuge System, as stated in the Improvement Act, is "to administer a national network of lands and waters for the conservation, management, and where appropriate, restoration of the fish, wildlife and plant resources and their habitats within the United States for the benefit of present and future generations of Americans" (16 USC 668dd et seq.).

The goals of the National Wildlife Refuge System are:

- To preserve, restore, and enhance in their natural ecosystems (when practicable) all species of animals and plants that are endangered or threatened with becoming endangered;
- To perpetuate the migratory bird resource;
- To preserve a natural diversity and abundance of fauna and flora on refuge lands; and
- To provide an understanding and appreciation of fish and wildlife ecology and the human role in the environment and to provide refuge visitors with high-quality, safe, wholesome, and enjoyable recreational experiences oriented toward wildlife to the extent these activities are compatible with the purposes for which the refuge was established.

The Service has adopted an ecosystem approach to resource management and has identified 52 ecosystem units within the United States. The Salinas River National Wildlife Refuge is situated in the Service's Southern California Ecoregion. The Draft Conceptual Management Approach for Southern California Ecoregion Goals can be obtained from the Service by request. Specific ecoregion goals relevant to the Salinas River National Wildlife Refuge are discussed in Chapter 3 of this CCP.

Legal and Policy Guidance for Management of National Wildlife Refuges. Individual refuges (refuge units) are guided by the mission and goals of the National Wildlife Refuge System (see preceding section) and by the designated purpose of the refuge unit as described in establishing legislation or executive orders, Service laws and policy, and international treaties. Key concepts guiding the System are contained in the Refuge Recreation Act of 1962, the National Wildlife Refuge System Administration Act of 1966, Title 50 of the Code of Federal Regulations, the Fish and Wildlife Service Manual, and, most recently, the Improvement Act.

The National Wildlife Refuge System is the only network of Federal lands administered first for the protection of wildlife. No use of a refuge may be allowed unless it is determined to be compatible with the refuge's purpose. A *compatible use* is a use that, in the sound professional judgment of the refuge manager, will not materially interfere with or detract from the fulfillment of the mission of the National Wildlife Refuge System or the purposes of the individual refuge unit. *Sound professional judgment* is further defined as a decision that is consistent with principles of fish and wildlife management and administration, available science and resources, and adherence with law. In this context, the Refuge Recreation Act of 1962 authorizes the Secretary of the Interior to administer refuges, hatcheries, and other conservation areas for recreational use when such uses do not interfere with the area's primary purpose.

The National Wildlife Refuge System Administration Act of 1966 provides guidelines and directives for administration and management of all areas in the System, including wildlife refuges, areas for the protection and conservation of fish and wildlife threatened with extinction, wildlife ranges, game ranges, wildlife management areas, and waterfowl production areas. This Act was amended in 1997 by passage of the Improvement Act, which includes a unifying mission statement for the National Wildlife Refuge System (see page 3), establishes new guidelines for determining compatible uses on refuges, and requires that each refuge be managed under a CCP developed in an open public process. Under the Improvement Act, all refuge units are required to have a CCP in place by the year 2012. The Improvement Act further states that wildlife conservation is the priority of National Wildlife Refuge System lands and that the Secretary of the Interior shall ensure that the biological integrity and diversity and the environmental health of refuge lands are maintained. In addition, the Improvement Act encourages partnerships with Federal and State agencies, Tribes, organizations, industry, and the general public.

The Improvement Act identifies six wildlife-dependent recreational uses as priorities: hunting, fishing, wildlife observation and photography, environmental education, and environmental interpretation. As expressed priorities of the National Wildlife Refuge System, these public uses take precedence over other potential uses in refuge planning and management. However, the Improvement Act also requires identification of existing compatible wildlife-dependent uses that will be permitted to continue on an interim basis pending completion of the CCP development process.

Refuge Vision. A vision statement is developed or revised for each individual refuge unit as part of the CCP process. Vision statements are grounded in the unifying mission of the National Wildlife Refuge System, and describe the desired future conditions of the refuge unit in the long term (more than 15 years), based on the refuge's specific purposes, the resources present on the refuge, and any other relevant mandates.

## The Salinas River National Wildlife Refuge
### Introduction to the Salinas River NWR
The Salinas River National Wildlife Refuge (hereafter, Refuge) encompasses 367 acres located 11 miles north of Monterey, California, where the Salinas River empties into Monterey Bay (Figures 1 and 2). The Refuge is part of the San Francisco Bay National Wildlife Refuge Complex, which has its headquarters in Fremont, California.

*Refuge Purpose: The Refuge was established in 1973 because of its "particular value in carrying out the national migratory bird management program" (16 USC Sec. 667b).*

Refuge lands include a range of terrestrial and aquatic habitats, including coastal dunes and beach, grasslands, wetlands, and riparian scrub. Because of its location within the Pacific Flyway, the Refuge is used by a variety of migratory birds during breeding, wintering, and migration periods. It also provides habitat for several threatened and endangered species, including western snowy plover, California brown pelican, Smith's blue butterfly, Monterey gilia, and Monterey spineflower. Approximately 40 species that occur or are suspected to occur on the Refuge are considered sensitive by Federal or State agencies (see Appendix C). Current recreational uses on the Refuge include wildlife observation and photography and access to surf fishing and waterfowl hunting. Chapter 4 presents a detailed description of natural resources on the Salinas River National Wildlife Refuge.

### Establishment and History of the Salinas River NWR
The Refuge was established in 1973 because of its "particular value in carrying out the national migratory bird management program" (16 USC Sec. 667b). The land was acquired by the Service through a transfer of surplus military land from the U.S. Army and the U.S. Coast Guard. From 1974 through 1991, what is now the Refuge was operated as a Wildlife Management Area under a cooperative agreement with the California Department of Fish and Game. By the mid-1980s, growing awareness of the Refuge's importance as habitat for sensitive species prompted a shift toward more active management and protection of its resources. In 1991, the Service began managing the area as a National Wildlife Refuge (NWR) under the National Wildlife Refuge System Administration Act of 1966, the Refuge Recreation Act of 1962, and the Improvement Act of 1997.

**Figure 1. Location Map**

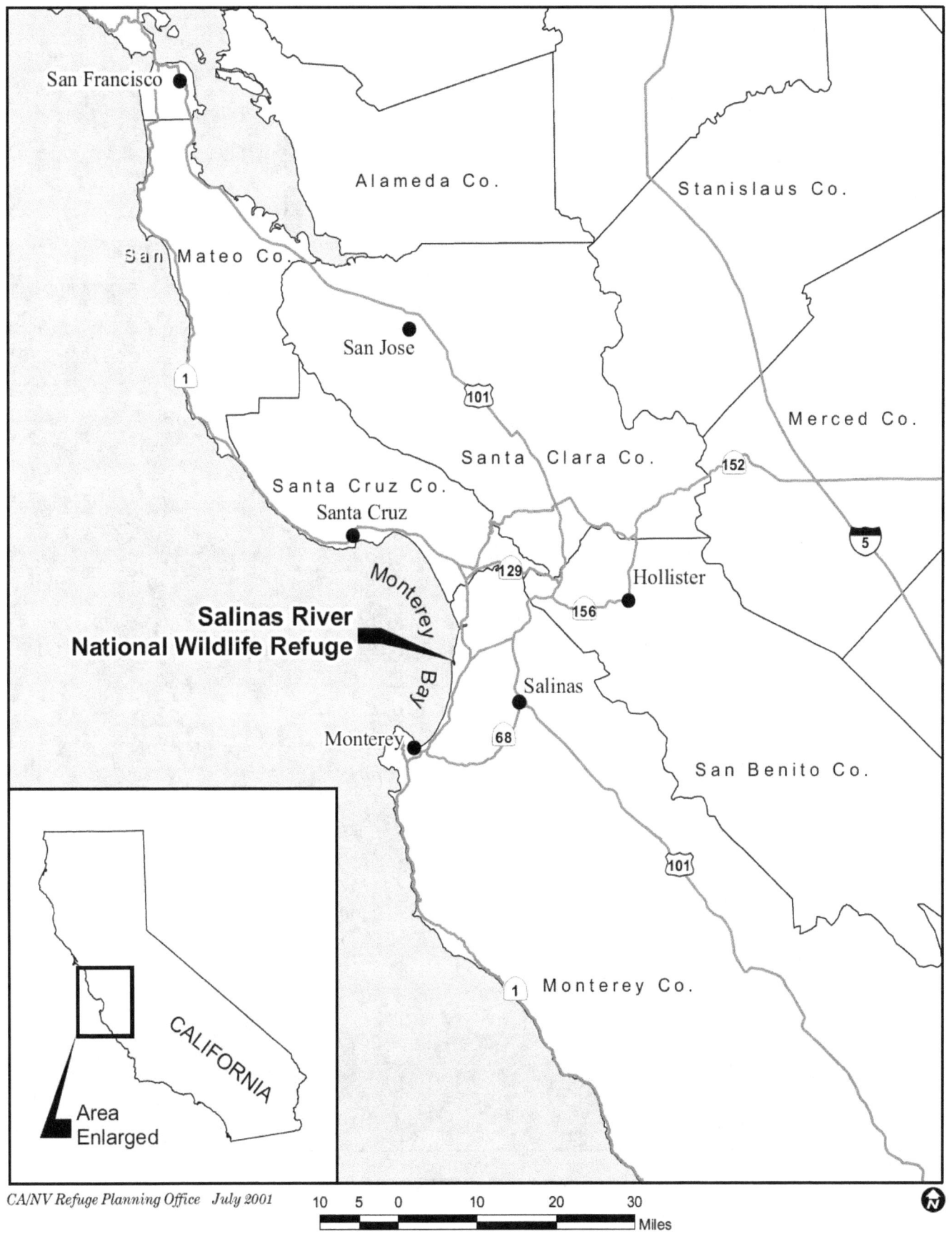

San Francisco ●

Alameda Co.

Stanislaus Co.

San Mateo Co.

San Jose ●

Merced Co.

Santa Cruz Co.

Santa Clara Co.

152

Santa Cruz ●

5

Monterey Bay

129

**Salinas River National Wildlife Refuge**

Hollister ●

156

Salinas ●

68

San Benito Co.

Monterey ●

CALIFORNIA

Area Enlarged

101

1   Monterey Co.

10   5   0   10   20   30

Miles

# Figure 2. Refuge Map

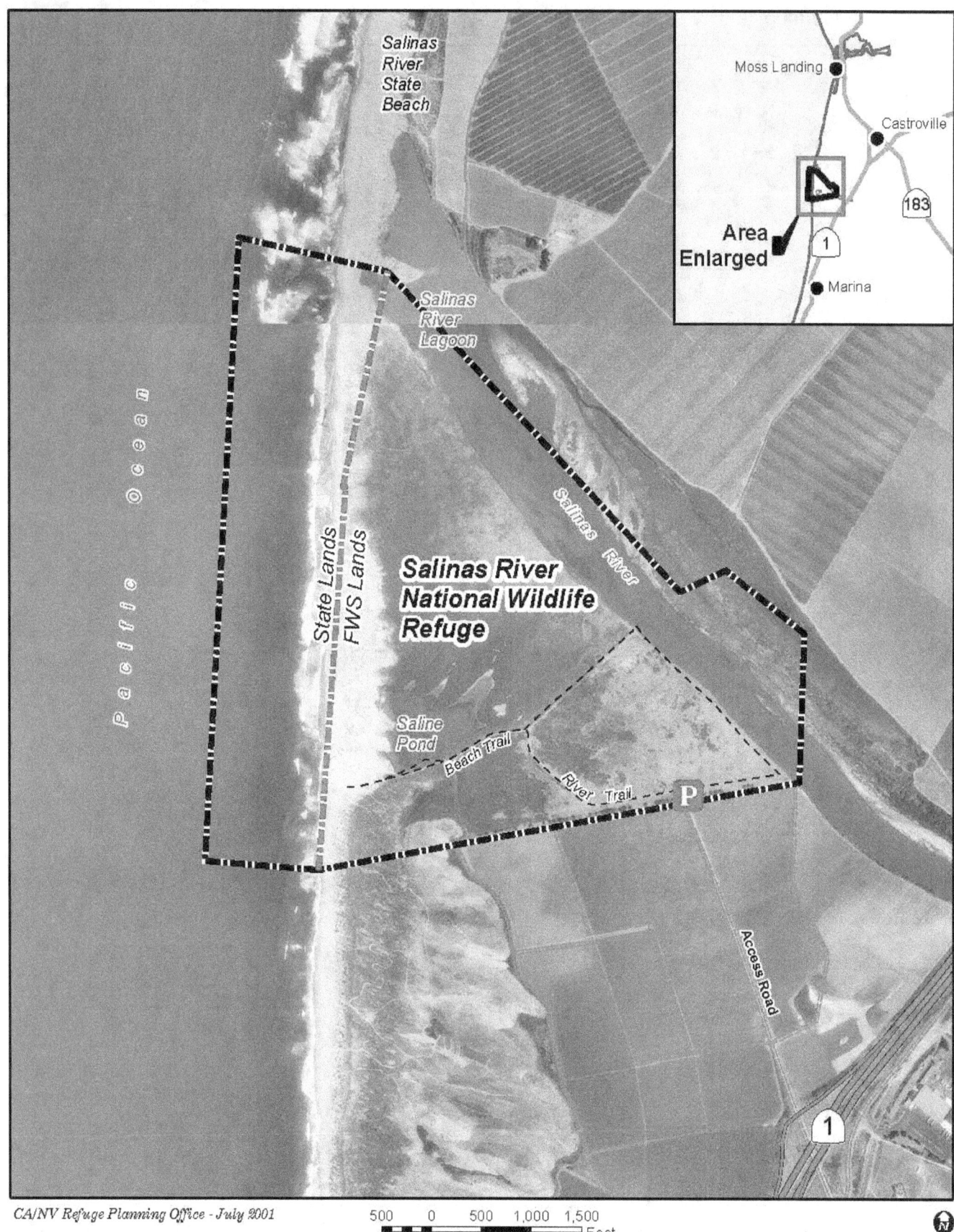

CA/NV Refuge Planning Office - July 2001

500 0 500 1,000 1,500 Feet

▬▪▬▪▬▪▪ Approved Refuge Boundary     ▬▬▪▬▪▬▪ State Lands / FWS Lands Boundary     P Parking Lot

Since 1991, Refuge management efforts have focused on sensitive species protection, habitat enhancement (including riparian restoration along the Salinas River), and public use management. Limited recreational opportunities have also been available to the public, including waterfowl hunting, access to surf fishing, and wildlife observation and photography. Much of the management and monitoring on the Refuge has been accomplished in cooperation with various partner organizations (see *Existing Partnerships* below). The Service's approach to managing the Refuge has been regional in perspective, and has emphasized balancing appropriate uses among the various public lands in the Monterey Bay area. Additional detailed information on past and current Refuge management is provided in Chapters 3 and 4.

### Salinas River NWR Vision Statement

This CCP incorporates the following vision statement for the Salinas River National Wildlife Refuge.

> The Refuge will be managed for the conservation and enhancement of populations of native species of plants, wildlife, fish, and their habitats. Endangered or threatened species will receive management priority, with special emphasis placed on the conservation and recovery of the western snowy plover. Whenever possible, habitats and populations will be managed in partnership with local landowners, local and regional organizations, and local, State, and other Federal agencies to achieve regional conservation goals.

The vision for the Refuge reflects the regional approach that the Service has taken since it began active management of the Refuge in 1991. Under this approach, the Refuge is viewed as part of a mosaic of different types of open spaces (State beaches, private lands, the Refuge, etc.) in the Monterey coastal region. Each type of open space may support different recreational uses that reflect the particular mission of the agency or entity with stewardship responsibility for those lands.

In keeping with this approach and with the mission of the National Wildlife Refuge System, the Refuge will continue to offer limited but unique wildlife-oriented recreational opportunities; however, significant increases in public use will not be encouraged. State and local beaches will continue to provide the primary recreational opportunities for the Monterey Bay area shoreline. State beaches in Monterey Bay typically offer opportunities for recreational activities—such as hang-gliding, camping, and horseback riding—that the Refuge does not allow. These uses, as well as unrestricted public use in general, are incompatible with the Refuge's purpose. The Refuge vision statement reflects the Service's view that, within the wider context of public lands along the Monterey Bay, the Refuge should support relatively undisturbed habitat for threatened and endangered species and other wildlife, where public uses are subordinate to the primary purpose of wildlife conservation.

Table 1 presents the 15-year vision for the Refuge's four primary habitats and for recreation.

**Table 1. 15-year vision for the primary habitats and for recreation on the Refuge.**

| | |
|---|---|
| Coastal Dunes and Beach | The natural processes of dune formation will be restored. Native vegetation in the dune complex of the Refuge will be protected and enhanced. Populations of endangered and threatened species such as Smith's blue butterfly, Monterey gilia, Monterey spineflower, brown pelican, and western snowy plover will be protected and enhanced. |
| Grassland | The native coastal prairie will be restored by mimicking natural processes through active management. The restored coastal prairie will provide excellent foraging habitat for native grassland birds. |
| Wetlands | The saline pond will be maintained for migratory bird use. The salt marsh habitat will be enhanced for use by migratory and resident birds. Historic wetlands on the Refuge will be identified and restored. |
| Riparian/Riverine Habitats | Riparian scrub will be restored along the Salinas River to provide habitat for migratory and resident birds while allowing for natural migration of the river channel. Riverine habitat will be enhanced for use by native waterfowl and fish. |
| Recreation | Limited wildlife dependent recreation will occur on the Refuge, when compatible with the purpose of the Refuge and the conservation and recovery of endangered species. |

*Management Goals for the Salinas River NWR*
Three goals have been identified to realize the vision proposed for the Refuge.

Goal 1. **Protect, restore, and enhance populations of migratory birds and other native species and their habitats.**

Goal 2. **Protect and enhance populations of endangered, threatened, and rare species and promote their recovery by restoring and enhancing their natural habitats.**

Goal 3. **Provide opportunities for safe, unique, wildlife-dependent recreation when compatible with the Refuge purpose and with other Refuge goals.**

These goals represent broad statements of the priorities for ongoing Refuge management.

*Existing Partnerships for Management of the Salinas River NWR*
Partnerships are integral to the success of many refuges, and the Service encourages partnerships with local organizations who share the Service's mission to conserve and enhance natural resources. The Refuge currently maintains partnerships with many organizations to help achieve its goals and those of the partner organizations. Table 2 summarizes current partnerships on the Refuge.

**Table 2. Current partnerships on the Salinas River National Wildlife Refuge.**

| *Organization* | *Nature of Partnership* |
| --- | --- |
| U.S. Department of Agriculture Wildlife Services | Assists with the Refuge's predator management program |
| California Department of Fish and Game | Coordinates programs for managing special status species, such as western snowy plover, on nearby State lands. |
| California Department of Parks and Recreation | Assists the Service with public use monitoring, habitat management, and snowy plover management |
| Watershed Institute of California State University, Monterey Bay | Conducts restoration of native grassland and riparian habitats, erosion monitoring, and scientific research |
| Point Reyes Bird Observatory | Conducts monitoring of western snowy plover populations |
| Santa Cruz Predatory Bird Research Group | Assists with the Refuge's experimental avian predator management program |
| Neighboring landowners | Control nonnative plants on dune habitat |

Source: Christopher Barr and Ivette Loredo, USFWS

## *Adaptive Management*

The Service acknowledges that much remains to be learned about the species, habitats, and physical processes that occur on the Refuge, and about the ecological interactions between species. When faced with uncertainty resulting from complex ecological interactions or gaps in available data, the most effective approach to resource management over the long term is an adaptive one. *Adaptive management* refers to a management style in which the effectiveness of management actions is monitored and evaluated, and future management is modified as needed, based on the results of this evaluation or other relevant information that becomes available. The Service has been practicing adaptive management on the Refuge since 1991 and plans to continue this practice. Accordingly, the management scenario proposed in this CCP provides for ongoing adaptive management of the Refuge; its adaptive management component is described more fully in Chapter 6, *Plan Implementation*.

## Document Organization

This document is organized into six chapters and eleven appendices. Table 3 summarizes their contents.

**Table 3. Organization of the Comprehensive Conservation Plan.**

| Document Section | Content |
| --- | --- |
| Chapter 1 | Description of CCP development process. Overview of mission and responsibilities of U.S. Fish and Wildlife Service and goals of National Wildlife Refuge System. Summary of history and vision of Salinas River NWR. |
| Chapter 2 | Summary of process for development of this CCP, including specific public concerns identified and addressed during CCP development. |
| Chapter 3 | Descriptions of current and future management of the Salinas River NWR. |
| Chapter 4 | Description of existing resources on the Salinas River NWR. |
| Chapter 5 | Overview of process for implementing this CCP. |
| Appendix A | List of references cited. |
| Appendix B | Glossary of technical terms. |
| Appendix C | List of special status plant and animal species with the potential to occur on the Salinas River NWR or in the surrounding area. |
| Appendix D | Matrix showing relationship between vegetation classification system used in this document and National Vegetation Classification System. |
| Appendix E | List of members of the Salinas River NWR CCP planning team and members of the team that prepared this document. |
| Appendix F | Overview of wilderness review process (process that establishes whether lands should be recommended to Congress for designation as wilderness and inclusion in the National Wilderness System) and results of wilderness review for Salinas River NWR. |
| Appendix G | Compatibility determinations (results of formal review of compatibility of proposed public uses with stated refuge purpose) for Salinas River NWR. |
| Appendix H | Salinas River NWR Avian Predator Management Plan (step down plan). |
| Appendix I | Salinas River NWR Wildland Fire Management Plan (step down plan). |
| Appendix J | Salinas River NWR Hunt Plan (step down plan). |
| Appendix K | Response to Comments |

# Chapter 2. The Comprehensive Conservation Planning Process

This CCP for the Salinas River National Wildlife Refuge is intended to meet the requirements of compliance with the Improvement Act[1]. The development of this CCP was also guided by the refuge planning policy outlined in Part 602, Chapters 1, 3, and 4 of the U.S. Fish and Wildlife Service Manual (May 2000).

Service policy, the Improvement Act, and the National Environmental Policy Act (NEPA) provide specific guidance for the planning process. For example, Service policy and NEPA require the Service to actively seek public involvement in the preparation of environmental documents such as Environmental Assessments (EAs). NEPA also requires the Service to give serious consideration to all reasonable alternatives, including the "no action" alternative, which represents continuation of current conditions and management practices. Alternative management scenarios were developed as part of the planning process described in this chapter.

## The Planning Process – How This CCP Was Developed
Key steps in the Service's CCP planning process include:
1. Forming the planning team and conducting preplanning;
2. Initiating public involvement and scoping;
3. Identifying issues and developing or revising vision and goal statements;
4. Developing alternatives and assessing their environmental effects;
5. Identifying the proposed action (i.e., the preferred alternative);
6. Publishing the draft plan and NEPA document;
7. Revising the draft plan and publishing a final plan; and
8. Implementing the plan.

Figure 3 diagrams the CCP planning process; the following sections provide additional detail on individual steps in the process.

### The Planning Team
The planning team responsible for leading the CCP effort included Service biologists, planners, and public use specialists from the San Francisco Bay NWR Complex and the California/Nevada Refuge Planning Office. Biologists and planners from Jones & Stokes, an environmental consulting firm, also participated in the planning team effort. This document was prepared by a technical team from Jones & Stokes, under the direction and with the assistance of the Service. Appendix E lists the members of the planning and technical teams.

---

[1]See discussion in Chapter 1.

### Figure 3. Comprehensive Conservation Planning Process

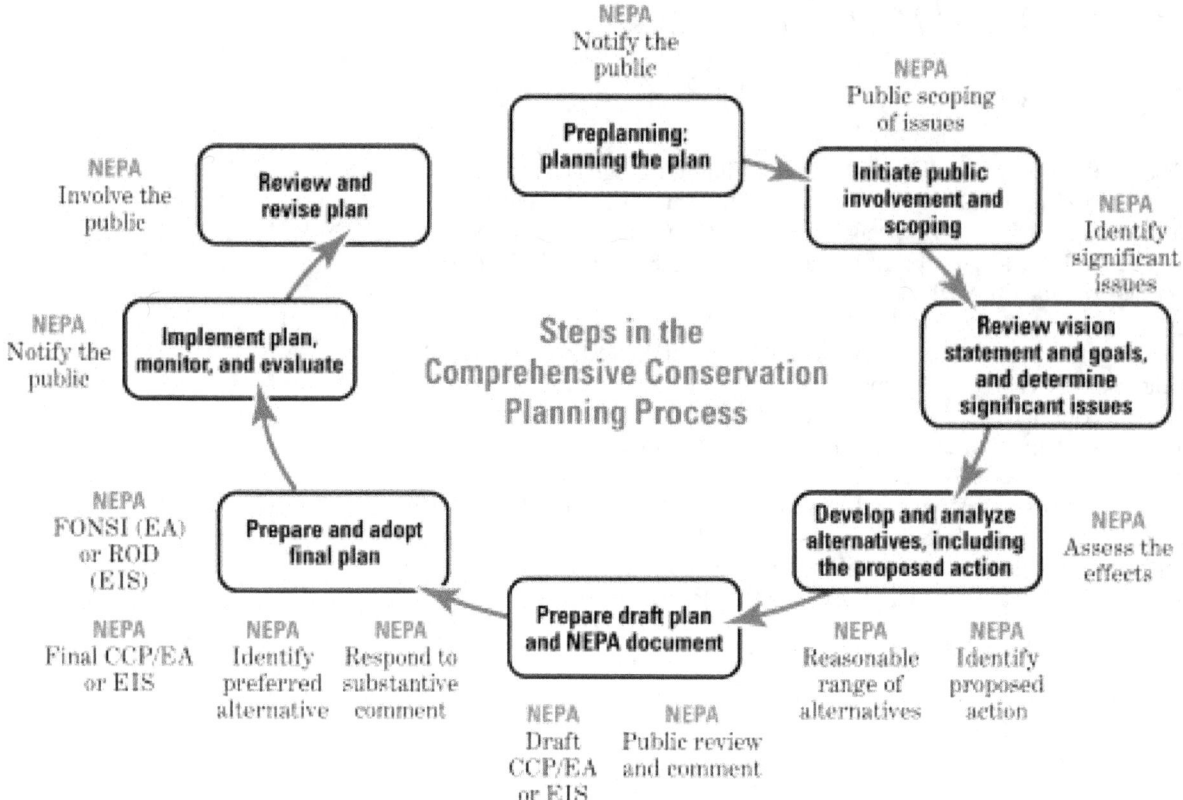

Coordination and cooperation among participating stakeholders was a fundamental element of the CCP development process. The Planning Team considered the interests and expertise of many agencies and organizations, including:

- U.S. Fish and Wildlife Service,
- California Department of Fish and Game,
- California Department of Parks and Recreation,
- Point Reyes Bird Observatory,
- Santa Cruz Predatory Bird Research Group,
- California State University, Monterey Bay Watershed Institute, and
- U.S. Department of Agriculture, Wildlife Services.

Project planning meetings attended by representatives of these entities were held regularly throughout the planning process, from November 1999 through July 2000. Issues, concerns, and opportunities were identified through discussions with planning team members and key contacts and through public involvement.

#### Public Involvement in Planning

Public involvement is an essential component of the CCP process. The Service announced the initiation of the Refuge planning effort to the public on May 19, 2000, through a planning update newsletter, followed by a formal notice in the Federal Register published on May 23, 2000. A press release was also issued prior to the public meeting.

**Public scoping meeting, Monterey, CA**
*Jones & Stokes Photo*

There were several avenues for public involvement in Refuge planning. A public workshop was held on June 1, 2000, in Monterey, California, to inform the public of the planning process, and written public comments were solicited until the public comment period ended on June 22, 2000.

## Public Comments on Refuge Planning

The following sections present issues, concerns, and opportunities summarized from all public input received during the scoping process. (The public workshop and written comment period are collectively referred to as the scoping process.)

### Recreation and Public Use

Public comments included concerns over recreation use, including both access issues and issues related to impacts. Some respondents felt that access to the portion of the Salinas River mouth below high tide should be prohibited. Concern was also expressed regarding the effects of human population density and recreational use on native plants and wildlife. Commentors suggested that snowy plover signage should be posted in English, Spanish, Chinese, and Tagalog. Some commentors suggested that signage prohibiting dogs should be clarified and increased. Others suggested that the Service issue a map showing areas in the Monterey region where dogs are allowed. Commentors recommended enhanced signage to identify areas of the Salinas River (both within and beyond the Refuge boundaries) where fishing is permitted. A desire for bilingual Spanish and English signage was expressed. Investigation into the impacts of hunting and other recreational activities on wildlife, such as disturbance of non-target species, was requested. The Service was also asked to consider the incompatibility of recreational hunting on the Refuge.

### Habitat and Wildlife Management

Many people were concerned about the loss of wildlife habitat and felt that protecting, restoring, and enhancing wildlife populations and habitats should be a Refuge priority. Development of a database of pertinent scientific information regarding habitats and wildlife on the Refuge was suggested. Some commentors recommended a rigorous biological assessment and inventory of all plant, fish, and wildlife species present on the Refuge, including birds and invertebrates. Respondents suggested that the Service consider the use of prescribed burning to restore grassland. Control of invasive species was also identified as a concern, and respondents recommended that additional approaches to avian predator management be considered, such as creating foraging habitat by mowing grassland. People stressed the need for long-term, effective, humane, and socially acceptable predator-management strategies. In addition, commentors expressed concern for the maintenance of good water quality on the Refuge.

*Administration and Management*

The Service received a variety of comments related to Refuge administration and management. Some comments suggest that the Refuge requires improved and additional publicity; many members of the public had not heard of the Refuge or the CCP process. Commentors recommended that the Service determine the CCP's consistency with other relevant programs and existing watershed and ecosystem efforts and ensure partnership with the California Department of Fish and Game. They also pointed out the need to comply with each requirement of the Refuge Administration Act, and to prioritize activities proposed in the CCP. Adoption of monitoring, evaluation, and adaptive management strategies was also suggested. Other commentors indicated a need for additional refuse receptacles at the Refuge, recommended that the access road be maintained as unpaved, suggested that the Refuge entrance and parking lot be moved to a location directly adjacent to the highway, and requested that areas in the Salinas River where fishing is allowed be clearly defined. Improved communication with local airports was also recommended, because low-flying airplanes and hang gliders have been spotted over the Refuge; commentors expressed concern about disturbance to wildlife. Participants expressed interest in identification of additional research opportunities. One respondent suggested that additional funding sources to support expanding the Refuge should be identified.

*Planning Process*

Some meeting participants recommended that mechanisms for providing a response to public comments be established.

## Development of Refuge Goals

The purpose of the Refuge is established by law; however, before this CCP effort, the Refuge had no vision statement. Under the Improvement Act, the task of the planning team was to revise and further develop the management focus of the Refuge within the Service's planning framework (Figures 3 and 4). Developing the new vision statement was given high priority because its description of desired future conditions on the Refuge helped guide the remainder of the planning process. The vision statement was based, in part, on the public comments received during the scoping period.  Once the vision statement was articulated, the planning team used it to examine and clarify the Refuge's three interim goals. The revised Refuge goals that resulted are presented in Chapter 1.

**Figure 4. Hierarchy of Refuge Planning Levels in the National Wildlife Refuge System**

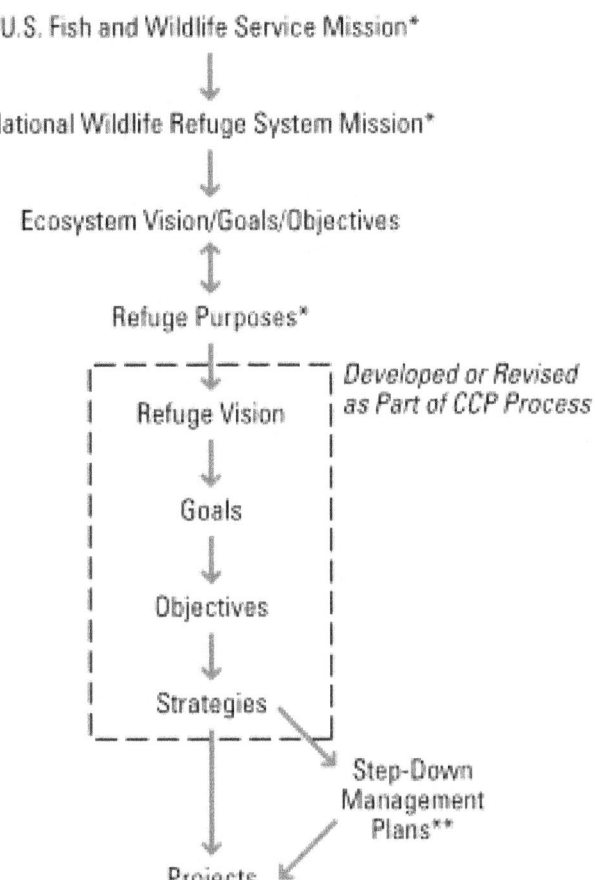

* Established by law.
** May be required to implement some projects; sometimes included in CCP.

### Development of Alternatives

The remaining steps in the CCP process, including development of alternatives, assessment of their environmental effects, and identification of the preferred management alternative (proposed action) were addressed in the EA (published as a CCP/EA).

### Plan Implementation

Chapter 5 describes the process for implementing the management plan proposed in this CCP.

# Chapter 3. Current and Future Refuge Management

**Wildlife monitoring**
*USFWS Photo*

## Current Management

The Refuge currently has no integrated plan to guide the management of all of its resources and uses. Current management efforts on the Refuge focus on the protection of sensitive species, the enhancement of their habitats, and the management of public access to and use of Refuge lands. A major emphasis of current management is the protection of the western snowy plovers by a variety of means, including: "Sensitive Wildlife Habitat – Closed Area" signs; nest exclosures; symbolic fencing (low cable fence used to keep humans from approaching nests); and law enforcement patrols. Western snowy plovers are monitored each breeding season for reproductive success and all chicks are banded for further monitoring. In addition, mammalian predators (including nonnative red foxes, feral cats, and skunks) are managed to selectively remove problem predators during the snowy plover breeding season. Black legless lizards are surveyed monthly using a standardized protocol. Coastal sand dune habitat on the Refuge is maintained by intensive hand-weeding and chemical control of invasive nonnative vegetation. Native grassland has been restored and is maintained by regular mechanical mowing and weed-whacking, and riparian restoration is an ongoing effort along the Salinas River.

Wildlife and habitat protection has been a clear management priority for the Refuge because of the National Wildlife Refuge System's conservation responsibility. Unrestricted or uncontrolled public use is not compatible with this mission nor with the purpose for which the Refuge was created. However, limited recreational opportunities have been available for the public on the Refuge, including waterfowl hunting, surf fishing access, and wildlife observation and photography. Because the State Lands Commission owns the land below mean high water, the Service cannot, under any alternative, prohibit public access to these tidal lands adjacent to the Refuge.

## Management Alternatives

In compliance with NEPA, four management alternatives were developed:

- Alternative 1: No Action,
- Alternative 2: Reduce Public Use and Improve and Expand Resource Management,
- Alternative 3: Improve Public Use and Resource Management, and
- Alternative 4: Expand and Improve Public Use and Resource Management.

See the Draft CCP/EA for a summary and description of these alternatives.

Following comprehensive review and analysis, the Service selected Alternative 3 as its proposed action for the Refuge because it is the alternative that the Service believes best meets the following criteria.

- Achieves the mission of the National Wildlife Refuge System.
- Is consistent with the Service's ecoregion goals.
- Achieves the purpose of the Salinas River National Wildlife Refuge.
- Will be able to achieve the 15-year vision and goals for the Refuge.
- Maintains and restores the ecological integrity of the habitats and populations on the Refuge.
- Addresses the important issues identified during the scoping process.
- Addresses the legal mandates of the Service and the Refuge.
- Addresses the legal mandates of the Service and the Refuge.
- Is consistent with the scientific principles of sound fish and wildlife management and endangered species recovery.

**Beach access trail**
*Jones & Stokes Photo*

Under Alternative 3, *Improve Public Use and Resource Management*, public use of the Refuge will be improved but not substantially expanded. For example, informational signs and interpretive exhibits will be installed on the Refuge. In addition, the existing parking lot will be improved (e.g., graded and covered with gravel or another pervious material). The area in which seasonal waterfowl hunting is permitted will be reduced by approximately 15% to protect roosting California brown pelicans (Figure 5).

All of the current management activities will continue. Some activities, such as special-status species inventories, will be substantially expanded. New management tools and techniques will include: use of prescribed fire to augment mowing and herbicide use in the grassland/shrubland habitat; inventories of all habitats on the Refuge; translocation of problem avian predators of the western snowy plover; and creation of a GIS database to track vegetation and population trends. In addition, the Service will pursue a long-term lease with the State Lands Commission so it can manage the beach and tidelands below mean high water. The selected management scenario is described in detail in the next section.

**Coastal sand dunes**
*USFWS Photo*

### Refuge Management Direction: Objectives and Strategies

Under the Improvement Act, specific management direction for NWRs is expressed in terms of objectives and strategies. As discussed in Chapter 1, refuge goals are broad, open-ended statements of refuge emphasis and direction. Refuge goals may or may not be feasible within the 15-year time frame of the CCP. In contrast, refuge objectives are concise statements of what will be achieved to help meet a particular refuge goal. When possible, refuge objectives should be measurable, clear, and specific, and should be feasible within the 15-year lifespan of the CCP. Refuge strategies describe specific actions or combinations of actions that can be used to meet an objective. In some cases, strategies describe specific projects in enough detail to assess funding and staffing needs. In other cases, further site-specific detail is required to implement a strategy; this usually takes the form of a step-down management plan (see Figure 4).

The three Refuge management goals stated in Chapter 1 are repeated below to provide the context for the proposed management direction. The objectives and strategies of this CCP are listed below as they apply to each of the three Refuge goals.

*Organization*

Each objective and each strategy is given a unique numeric code for easy reference. Objectives have a two-digit code (e.g., 1.1, 1.2, 2.1, 2.2). The first digit corresponds to the goal to which the objective applies. The second digit is sequential and corresponds approximately to the priority given to that objective relative to others under the same goal. Similarly, each strategy has a three-digit code (e.g., 1.1.1, 1.1.2, 2.1.1, 2.1.2). The first and second digits refer to the appropriate goal and objective, respectively. The third digit is sequential; it indicates priority only for actions with deadlines. Strategies are sometimes also grouped by subtopic.

*Goals, Objectives, and Strategies*

**Goal 1.0.** **Protect, restore, and enhance populations of migratory birds and other native species and their habitats**

*Objective 1.1:*
*By 2017, the Refuge will restore native riparian vegetation along at least 1,500 feet of the south bank of the Salinas River to increase the density and diversity of migratory and resident songbirds on the Refuge.*

Rationale: Protection and enhancement of riparian habitat, coastal lagoons, and estuaries is a major ecoregional goal. The Salinas River is specifically identified as a priority site in *The Riparian Bird Conservation Plan* (RHJV 2000), and recommendations therein will guide habitat restoration efforts along the river. Promoting structural diversity and volume of the understory and to restoring the width of the riparian corridor will be of primary importance. In addition to enhancing productivity of riparian-dependent birds, riparian restoration efforts will improve conditions for native fish by shading and cooling the water's edge. Restoration should also help slow erosion of the river bank. Special consideration will be given to habitat needs of USFWS Birds of Conservation Concern that are included on the Pacific Region and Coastal California Bird Conservation lists (hereafter, Birds of Conservation Concern) (see Table C-2 in Appendix C).

| Objective 1.1 – Restore Native Riparian Vegetation | |
|---|---|
| *Code* | *Strategy* |
| Restore Native Riparian Vegetation | |
| 1.1.1 | Continue to plant and maintain riparian trees and shrubs native to the lower Salinas River along the riverbank using cuttings from upstream populations; focus on improving structural diversity and corridor width and maintaining dense shrub and herbaceous layer vegetation. Continue to provide support to partners such as the Watershed Institute of CSU Monterey Bay to implement this strategy. |
| 1.1.2 | Work with restoration partners to develop by 2005 a long-term monitoring strategy to evaluate the survival and density of riparian revegetation. |
| 1.1.3 | Evaluate the erosion of the south bank of the Salinas River and the effectiveness of riparian restoration in stabilizing this erosion by monitoring its location using Global Positioning System equipment. These data will be entered into the Refuge GIS database. |
| 1.1.4 | By 2010, establish a program to monitor the response of migratory and resident bird populations to riparian restoration on the Refuge. Work with staff from the Service's Migratory Bird and Habitat Programs to develop the monitoring strategy, and foster partnerships with nonprofit groups such as the Ventana Wilderness Society to help implement this strategy. |

# Figure 5.  Public Use Plan

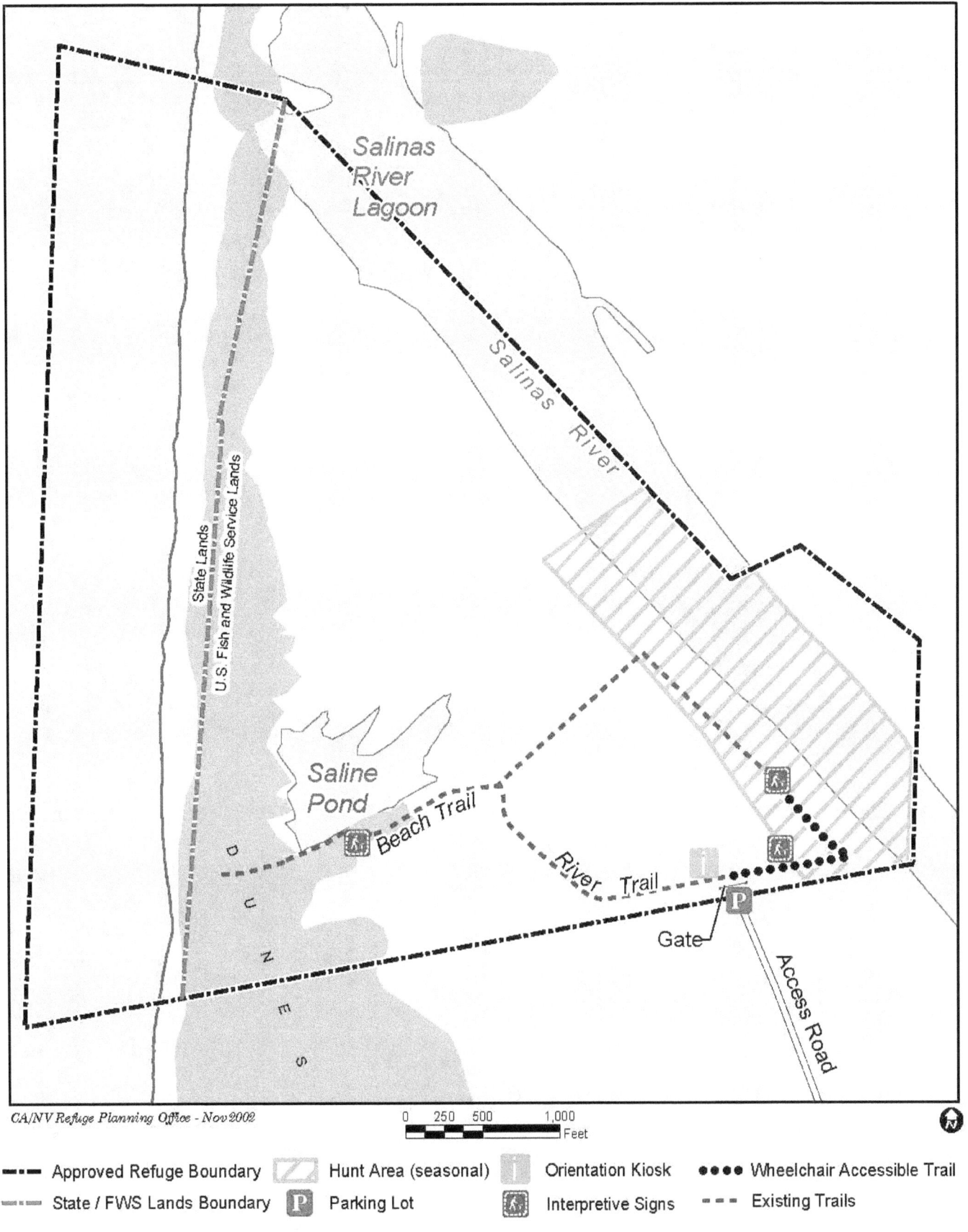

Salinas River Lagoon

Salinas River

State Lands

U.S. Fish and Wildlife Service Lands

Saline Pond

Beach Trail

River Trail

Gate

Access Road

D U N E S

0    250    500    1,000
Feet

-··-·· Approved Refuge Boundary      Hunt Area (seasonal)    Orientation Kiosk    ●●●● Wheelchair Accessible Trail

-··-·· State / FWS Lands Boundary    P Parking Lot    Interpretive Signs    - - - Existing Trails

*Objective 1.2:*
*Within the mosaic of grassland and northern coastal scrub*
*habitat, the Refuge will maintain between 50% and 75% cover of*
*native grassland composed of at least 90% (by plant cover) grasses*
*and herbs native to the local area.*

Rationale: Although extensive in the past, native grassland is now
a rare plant community and wildlife habitat in California.
Historically, native grasslands were naturally maintained by
recurring fires that prevented conversion to shrub-dominated
habitats. Since the end of agricultural operations on the Refuge in
the 1980s, shrubs have been slowly invading the grassland in the
absence of fire to suppress them. By maintaining a majority of the
shrubland/grassland mosaic in native grassland habitat, the
Refuge will likely retain this important habitat in sufficient
quantity to maintain the diversity of wildlife that now inhabits the
Refuge, and perhaps attract additional grassland- or shrub-
dependent species. Special consideration will be given to habitat
needs of Birds of Conservation Concern. Prescribed burns will
initially be used to restore and enhance the native grassland;
burning to control nonnative weeds will be conducted for several
consecutive years. Once nonnative species are reduced to
controllable levels in a given area, fire will then be used for
maintenance of the grasslands, requiring only periodic burns.

| Objective 1.2 – Maintain Native Grassland and Coastal Scrub | |
|---|---|
| *Code* | *Strategy* |
| Enhance Native Grassland | |
| 1.2.1 | Continue to mow the grassland annually and apply herbicide to control invasive plants such as poison hemlock and wild radish. |
| 1.2.2 | By 2004, initiate a prescribed burn program on the Refuge as an additional management tool (to augment mowing and herbicide use) for the enhancement and maintenance of native grassland. *See Appendix I for the Draft Wildland Fire Management Plan.* |
| 1.2.3 | By 2005, inventory and quantify the composition of the grassland on the Refuge. This inventory will include documenting historical land use of the grassland and the methodology and results of past restoration efforts. |

*Objective 1.3:*
*The Refuge will maintain and enhance its wetland and aquatic*
*habitat.*

Rationale: Protection and enhancement of wetlands is a major
ecoregional goal. The saline pond is a unique resource on the
Refuge that is important habitat for shorebirds such as American
avocet, black-necked stilt, and other water birds. Increasing
breeding populations of snowy plover, black-necked stilt, and
American avocet by enhancing, restoring, or creating nesting
habitat is a conservation priority identified in the National and
Southern Pacific Coast Regional Shorebird Plans. The aquatic
habitat of the Salinas River Lagoon is a unique regional resource
that provides cover and food for a diverse assemblage of fish,
insects, invertebrates, and waterfowl, as well as terns, osprey, and
muskrat. The lagoon supports several special-status species,
including steelhead (federally listed as threatened). The Salinas
River is also the only habitat in which hunting is now permitted on
the Refuge. Special consideration will be given to the habitat
needs of Birds of Conservation Concern.

| Objective 1.3 – Maintain and Enhance Wetland and Aquatic Habitats | |
|---|---|
| *Code* | *Strategy* |
| Enhance Wetland and Aquatic Habitats | |
| 1.3.1 | By 2005, conduct a hydrologic study of the Refuge that includes quantifying the water balance of the saline pond, conducting water quality testing of the pond, and determining the possible sources of any contaminants in the pond. |
| 1.3.2 | By 2005, determine the historic extent of wetlands on the Refuge and the potential to restore degraded wetlands. |
| 1.3.3 | By 2010, complete a 2-year inventory of the species present in the Salinas River Lagoon. |
| 1.3.4 | Manage the saline pond for black-necked stilts, American avocets, and other shorebirds, as well as waterfowl, other water birds, and other species that depend on this habitat. |
| 1.3.5 | Continue to coordinate with the California Coastal Commission (CCC), National Marine Fisheries Service (NMFS), and the Service's Endangered Species Division regarding breaching of the Salinas River mouth by the Monterey County Water Resources Agency. If, in the future, this activity is proposed for lands owned or leased by the Service, a special use permit from the Service and continued consultation with the CCC would be required. |

*Objective 1.4:*
*The Refuge will enhance the coastal dune habitat for a diversity of native species.*

Rationale: Enhancement of coastal dune habitats is a major ecoregional goal. A majority of the Refuge's listed and special-status species occur in or near coastal dune scrub. Enhancing this habitat will benefit these species, including Smith's blue butterfly, black legless lizard, Monterey gilia, and Monterey spineflower. Special consideration will be given to the habitat needs of Birds of Conservation Concern. Removing and controlling invasive plants is critical to enhancement efforts because of their ability to spread rapidly and quickly displace native plants and wildlife (Pickart and Sawyer 1998).

**After a prescribed burn on a national wildlife refuge**
*J&K Hollingsworth Photo*

| Objective 1.4 – Enhance Coastal Dune Habitat | |
|---|---|
| *Code* | *Strategy* |
| Enhance Coastal Dune Scrub | |
| 1.4.1 | Maintain and enhance partnerships with State Parks to share information and coordinate monitoring to cooperatively and consistently manage coastal dune habitat. |
| 1.4.2 | Implement techniques to control invasive plants, using a combination of chemical and mechanical means. Chemical control may be conducted only during the non-breeding season (October through March). Hand-pulling may be conducted year-round in the backdunes, but only during October–March in the foredunes, where plovers nest. The method to be used will be determined by weed infestation size, potential for habitat disturbance, effects on non-target species, and efficiency. |

Note: Strategies 2.1.2, 2.1.3, 2.1.7, 2.1.8, 2.1.9, 2.3.1, and 2.3.2 also help to achieve this objective.

**Goal 2.0. Protect and enhance populations of endangered, threatened, and rare species, and promote their recovery by restoring and enhancing their natural habitats**

*Objective 2.1:*
*The Salinas River NWR will implement management actions to protect, conserve, and enhance populations of special-status species on the Refuge. Priority will be given to species that are state- or federally listed, are proposed for listing, or are candidates for listing.*

Rationale: The Service manages endangered and threatened species as trust species. Thus, the Service is responsible for assisting in the recovery of endangered and threatened species that occur within the refuge system. In order to implement effective active management for the protection and recovery of endangered and threatened species, a major goal of the refuge system overall and within the southern California ecoregion is to develop priorities for refuge management among species. Prioritization is important because limitations in funding and staff time prevent targeting all special-status species for management. Limited resources are allocated, in part, through inventories of special-status species and prioritization of management needs.

| Objective 2.1 – Protect Populations of Endangered, Threatened, and Rare Species | |
|---|---|
| *Code* | *Strategy* |
| Mapping, Species Inventories, and Monitoring | |
| 2.1.1 | By 2004, develop a Geographic Information System (GIS) database for the Refuge and overlay vegetation and wildlife habitat types. This database will be used to record locations of special-status species and to track habitat management actions, restoration projects, and maintenance actions. |
| 2.1.2 | By 2005, complete a 2-year inventory of the special-status species that occur on the Refuge. This inventory will include mapping the distribution and estimating the size of all populations of special-status species. Inventories will consist of field surveys and literature searches for historical records of special-status species. Locations of special-status species will be entered in the GIS database. |
| 2.1.3 | After completion of the 2-year baseline inventory of species on the Refuge, develop and implement a long-term monitoring program that tracks the effects of management actions and public use on special-status species. Monitoring data will be stored in the Refuge's GIS database. |
| 2.1.4 | By 2008, evaluate and prioritize the special-status species that occur on the Refuge to determine which species require active management and the level and type of management needed. Criteria for prioritization will include: listing status, implementation of actions identified in Recovery Plans, status in the Monterey Bay area, taxonomic distinctiveness, population size on the Refuge, threats to survival, sensitivity to disturbance, and the ability of the Refuge to contribute to recovery or conservation of the species. |
| Management and Research | |
| 2.1.5 | Encourage research on each priority special-status species on the Refuge to determine its ecology relevant to conservation. Research could be conducted by local universities or other organizations with assistance from the Refuge in the form of funding, supplies, volunteers, or technical assistance. |
| 2.1.6 | By 2006 (assuming additional lands are acquired), establish a satellite Refuge office in Monterey or Santa Cruz County to permit more efficient management of the two Monterey Bay area National Wildlife Refuges. Currently, Refuge staff are headquartered 80 miles away in Fremont, and a significant amount of time is spent commuting to and from the Refuge. *This strategy will assist the Refuge in achieving all of the goals and objectives in this CCP.* |
| 2.1.7 | By 2010, develop habitat management strategies to preserve and enhance populations of high-priority special-status species on the Refuge. These strategies will include detailed prescriptions for habitat management, protocols to monitor the status of these species, and methods to evaluate the effectiveness of management actions. The impacts of public use on special-status species will also be monitored. The strategies will cover federally listed species such as the California brown pelican, Smith's blue butterfly, Monterey gilia, and Monterey spineflower, and high-priority special-status species such as the black legless lizard. |

Note: Strategies 2.2.2, 2.2.3, 2.2.7, and 2.2.8 also help to achieve this Objective.

*Objective 2.2:*
*The Salinas River NWR will enhance the population of the western snowy plover on the foredunes of the Refuge so that by 2017 the snowy plover produces at least 1.0 fledged chick per male and there is at least 35 acres of high-quality breeding habitat for the plover.*

Rationale: The western snowy plover relies heavily on coastal beaches from southern Washington to Baja California for food, shelter, and raising its young. The Pacific coast populations of this species have been declining dramatically over the past decade because of substantial habitat loss related to industrial, urban, and recreational development, human disturbance, and encroachment of exotic vegetation. The coastal population of western snowy plover was listed as threatened by the U.S. Fish and Wildlife Service in 1993 (U.S. Fish and Wildlife Service 1993b).

Historically, the Monterey Bay area has supported one of the most productive populations of western snowy plovers on the central California coast (Page pers. comm.). Populations of snowy plovers in the Monterey Bay area have been dramatically reduced as a result of habitat loss and disturbance by thousands of beach visitors in summer. Since 1986, there has been a dramatic decline in plover nest success at the Refuge and on adjacent lands (see Chapter 4). Nonetheless, the plover breeding colony on and near the Refuge is one of California's most important, and protection of this resource is considered essential to the continued success of the species.

The strategies outlined to achieve this objective are consistent with the goals of the Draft Recovery Plan for the snowy plover recently released by the Service (U.S. Fish and Wildlife Service 2001). Achieving a fledge rate of at least 1.0 chick per male will provide a modest regional growth rate for plovers. This figure is based on the best available scientific information. During 1996–2000, the nest hatch rate on the Refuge was 67% and the chick fledge rate was 22%, with an average of 23.6 nests recorded per year. There is currently approximately 20 acres of high-quality nesting habitat for the plover on the Refuge. Maintaining at least 35 acres of suitable habitat for the plover on the Refuge would also ensure modest growth of the plover population on the Refuge. The population of plovers on the Refuge could become a "source" population (a population growing at a rate that is more than self-supporting) for plovers in the Monterey Bay area (Monterey Bay Area Snowy Plover Working Group 1999). Adult plovers on the Refuge have the potential to produce juveniles that could colonize new sites in the area or supplement existing populations elsewhere that are not self-supporting. Achieving this objective would help meet recovery goals for the western snowy plover (U.S. Fish and Wildlife Service 2001). Strategies that will implement specific recovery plan tasks are noted. Strategies for controlling invasive plans and minimizing disturbance to plovers should also benefit other nesting or winter shorebirds on the Refuge.

**Western snowy plover chick (*Charadrius alexandrinus nivosus*) on the Salinas River NWR**
*USFWS Photo*

| Objective 2.2 – Enhance Western Snowy Plover Population | |
|---|---|
| Code | Strategy |
| **Facilitate Regional Management** | |
| 2.2.1 | Continue to facilitate regular meetings of the Monterey Bay Area Snowy Plover Working Group to share information and develop successful management strategies to increase the population and geographic extent of snowy plovers throughout the Monterey Bay area. (Recover Plan task 3.1.1.) |
| 2.2.2 | Continue partnership with Point Reyes Bird Observatory to monitor snowy plover reproductive success on the Refuge. Each nest will be closely monitored and data will be collected on adult breeding population size, hatch rates, and fledge rates. All snowy plover chicks will be banded in order to collect information on survival and movement patterns. (Recovery Plan task 1.1.) |
| **Control Invasive Plants** | |
| 2.2.3 | Remove all European beach grass, iceplant, and other invasive plants from the foredunes of the Refuge by 2017. Control invasive plants in fall and winter (outside the plover breeding season) using chemical and mechanical means such as herbicide spraying, hand pulling, or heavy equipment. Techniques will be chosen based on their likelihood of success, their financial and labor costs, and their low potential for adverse environmental effects. (Recovery Plan task 1.2.5.1.) |
| **Minimize Human Disturbance in Nesting Habitat** | |
| 2.2.4 | Install clearer 'closed area' signs at the boundary of sensitive dune habitat by 2003. These signs should be similar to signs used at other plover nesting sites in the region. Install entrance signs, both at the parking lot and at the northern and southern beach access points, that clearly state that dogs and horses are not allowed on the Refuge (except dogs when hunting). (Recovery Plan tasks 1.3.1, 1.3.3, and 2.2.2.) |
| 2.2.5 | Develop and implement a docent program on the Refuge by 2006, in coordination with other agencies, to educate Refuge users during the sensitive breeding season on the ecology of western snowy plovers and the sensitivity of their habitat and nests to disturbance. (Recovery Plan tasks 5.4 and 5.5.) |
| 2.2.6 | Design and install interpretive signs at the entrance to and along the coastal dune trail by 2007 that explain to visitors the ecology of the western snowy plover and the plover's sensitivity to disturbance. Coordinate with other agencies to design interpretive signs with a message that is consistent with interpretive signs for snowy plovers at other sites in the Monterey Bay area. (Recovery Plan tasks 5.1, 5.3, and 5.4.) |
| 2.2.7 | By 2005, install symbolic fencing along beach trail around plover nests likely to be disturbed by the public; if trespass into closed areas continues, install symbolic fencing along the edge of foredune habitat to delineate sensitive areas and restrict human access. (Recovery Plan tasks 1.3.1 and 2.2.2.) |
| 2.2.8 | Increase enforcement of the closed dune habitat by increasing the presence of Service staff and law enforcement officers on the Refuge to at least one day per week each (two person-days per week) during the plover breeding season. (Recovery Plan tasks under 1.3 as well as 2.2.2, 2.2.3, and 2.2.4.) |
| 2.2.9 | Negotiate a long-term lease with the State Lands Commission to manage the beach, foredunes, and tidelands immediately west of the current boundary. (Recovery Plan tasks 1.3.1 and 2.2.2.) |
| **Control Predators on Eggs and Chicks** | |
| 2.2.10 | Continue to implement the Monterey Predator Management Program* on the Refuge to control predation on western snowy plovers by mammals. This program uses humane and target species–specific methods to control problem mammalian predators, primarily red foxes, feral cats, and skunks. Nonlethal methods (e.g., box-type traps, soft-catch padded leghold traps, hazing, bow nets, lures) will be used whenever possible. Lethal methods, including shooting and euthanasia, will be used when necessary. The Service will continue to coordinate this effort with other agencies such as the California Departments of Parks and Recreation and Fish and Game, and the U.S. Department of Agriculture Wildlife Services. (Recovery Plan tasks 1.4.3. and 1.4.4.) |
| 2.2.11 | Revise the Goals in the Refuge's Predator Management Plan to the following: "Maintain a 5-year productivity of at least 1.0 fledged chick per male and 40 breeding adults to reflect best available scientific information on requirements for achieving a self-sustaining population." |

| Objective 2.2 – Enhance Western Snowy Plover Population (*continued*) | |
|---|---|
| Facilitate Regional Management | |
| 2.2.12 | Implement the Avian Predator Management Plan to provide for removal and relocation of individual American kestrels, northern harriers, loggerhead shrikes, crows, ravens, and other problem avian predators that threaten nesting western snowy plovers on the Refuge and adjacent lands (see Appendix H for details of this proposed new project). (Recovery Plan tasks 1.4.2. and 1.4.4.) |

\* The details of the current Predator Management Program have been described and the environmental effects of this program evaluated in a previous plan (U.S. Fish and Wildlife Service 1993a). This plan and the associated NEPA document are available from the Service upon request.

*Objective 2.3:*
*The Refuge will protect and will encourage protection of as much of the coastal sand dune ecosystem in the Monterey Bay area as possible.*

Rationale: Protection and enhancement of coastal dune habitats is a major ecoregional goal and an important recovery action for the federally listed species that inhabit them. The coastal dune ecosystem is a rare habitat in California and is under increasing threats from development, off-highway vehicle use, and invasive plants. The dune system in the Monterey Bay area is among those in the State threatened by these factors (Big Sur Land Trust 1992). Coastal dunes north of the Refuge are largely protected by State parks and an ecological reserve (Figure 6). However, dunes south of the Refuge are largely unprotected; most dunes are privately owned within the cities of Marina, Sand City, Seaside, or Monterey. A 67% undivided interest in the Martin Dunes site, immediately south of the Refuge, was purchased in 2000 by the Big Sur Land Trust; several large private parcels between the Martin Dunes property and Marina State Beach support sand mining operations (California Department of Conservation 1992). The majority of these parcels remain undeveloped and encompass important coastal dune habitat that supports many listed species (California Department of Conservation 1992; Big Sur Land Trust 1992).

The endangered Smith's blue butterfly (*Euphilotes enoptes smithi*)

| Objective 2.3 – Protect Coastal Sand Dune Ecosystem | |
| --- | --- |
| *Code* | *Strategy* |
| Protect Coastal Sand Dune Ecosystem | |
| 2.3.1 | Establish partnerships with other landowners of coastal dune habitat to manage this habitat for conservation (e.g., controlling invasive plants on coastal dunes) through cooperative agreements, conservation easements, or financial incentives such as funding through the Partners for Wildlife program. The Service could also provide technical assistance, volunteer labor, financial assistance, or supplies to landowner partners. |
| 2.3.2 | Explore expansion of the current Refuge boundary by initiating the Service's planning process for expanding refuges, which culminates with a Land Protection Plan, Conceptual Management Plan, and NEPA document. |

*Goal 3.0.* **Provide opportunities for safe, unique, wildlife-dependent recreation when compatible with the purpose and goals of the Refuge**

*Objective 3.1:*
*The Refuge will provide limited opportunities for hunting and access to fishing when they are compatible with the purpose of the Refuge and refuge goals.*

Rationale: Hunting and fishing were identified in the Improvement Act as priority uses for refuges when they are compatible with refuge purposes. As a result, the Service encourages hunting and fishing on many NWRs. Because waterfowl hunting opportunities are limited in the Monterey Bay area (see Chapter 4), the Salinas River National Wildlife Refuge provides an important regional recreational opportunity for waterfowl hunters, and is unique in the area in providing opportunities for walk-in hunting (see Chapter 4). Hunting must be limited on the Refuge because of its importance to special-status species that are sensitive to disturbance. For example, the California brown pelican roosts near the current hunt area (see Chapter 4).

California brown pelicans (*Pelecanus occidentalis*)
*USFWS Photo*

# Figure 6.  Coastal Dunes and Land Ownership along Southern Monterey Bay

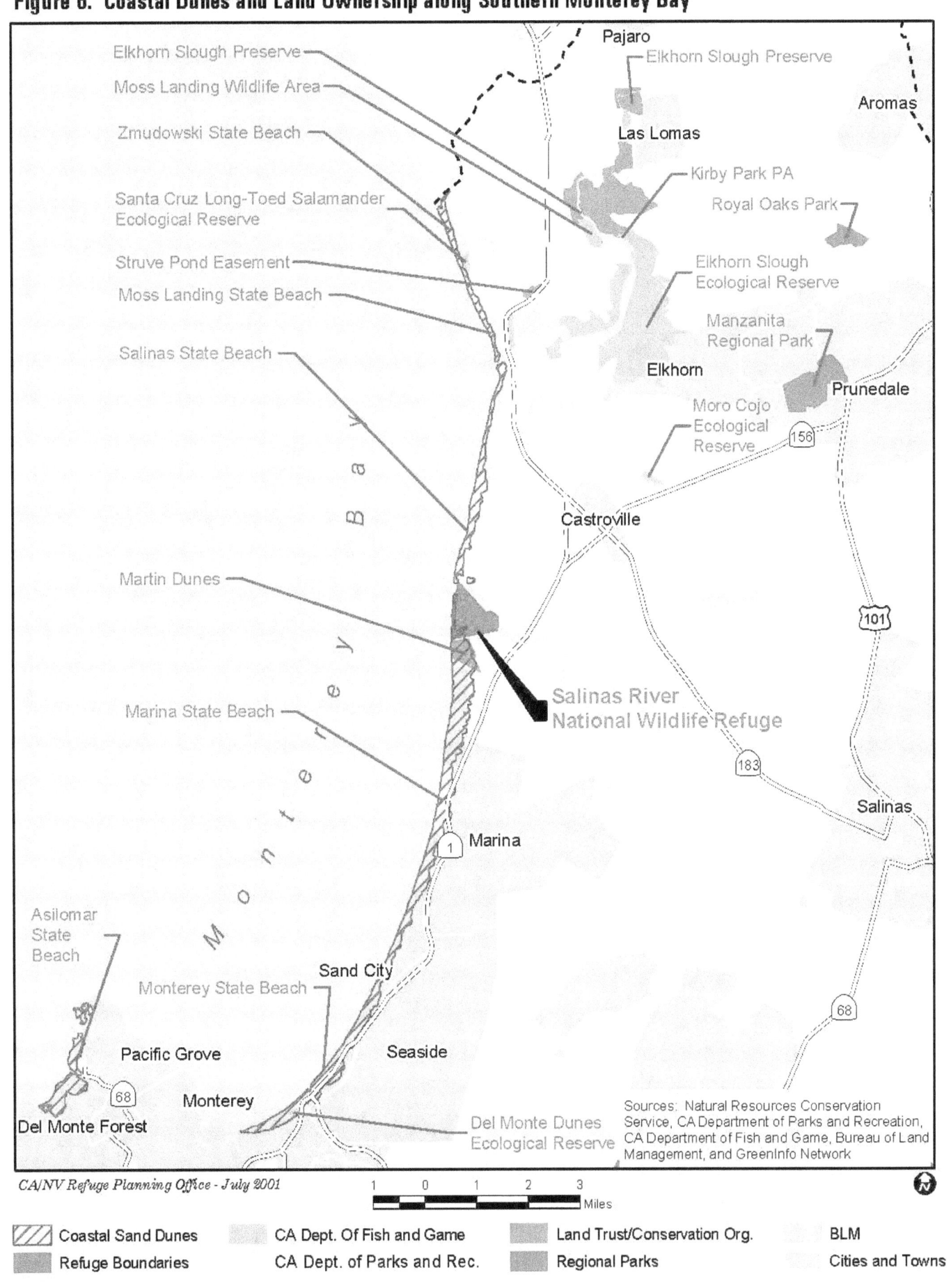

Pajaro

Elkhorn Slough Preserve

Aromas

Elkhorn Slough Preserve

Moss Landing Wildlife Area

Las Lomas

Zmudowski State Beach

Kirby Park PA

Royal Oaks Park

Santa Cruz Long-Toed Salamander
Ecological Reserve

Elkhorn Slough
Ecological Reserve

Struve Pond Easement

Manzanita
Regional Park

Moss Landing State Beach

Elkhorn

Prunedale

Salinas State Beach

Moro Cojo
Ecological
Reserve

156

Castroville

Martin Dunes

101

Salinas River
National Wildlife Refuge

Marina State Beach

183

Salinas

Marina

1

Asilomar
State
Beach

Sand City

68

Monterey State Beach

Pacific Grove

Seaside

68

Monterey

Del Monte Dunes
Ecological Reserve

Sources: Natural Resources Conservation
Service, CA Department of Parks and Recreation,
CA Department of Fish and Game, Bureau of Land
Management, and GreenInfo Network

Del Monte Forest

Monterey Bay

*CA/NV Refuge Planning Office - July 2001*

1   0   1   2   3

Miles

| | Coastal Sand Dunes | | CA Dept. Of Fish and Game | | Land Trust/Conservation Org. | BLM |
| Refuge Boundaries | | CA Dept. of Parks and Rec. | | Regional Parks | Cities and Towns |

| Objective 3.1 – Provide Fishing and Waterfowl Hunting Access or Opportunities | |
|---|---|
| *Code* | *Strategy* |
| **Hunting Opportunities** | |
| 3.1.1 | Reduce the hunting area on the Refuge from approximately 45 acres to approximately 38 acres (Figures 2 and 5) to reduce disturbance to pelicans roosting on the Refuge's island in the Salinas River. Clearly delineate hunt area with signs. |
| 3.1.2 | Annually monitor hunting use of the Refuge beginning in 2004. The information gathered will be used to review and possibly revise Refuge hunting regulations to enhance the quality and safety of the Refuge's hunting program. |
| **Surf Fishing Opportunities** | |
| 3.1.3 | Continue to provide access to opportunities for surf fishing between the high tide and surf zones. |

*Objective 3.2:*
*The Refuge will provide opportunities for wildlife observation and photography that will enable visitors to experience and enjoy the wildlife of the Refuge and develop an appreciation for wildlife species and their unique habitats.*

Rationale: The Improvement Act identified wildlife observation and wildlife photography as priority public uses for NWRs. Because these public uses are often compatible with wildlife management goals, the Service encourages wildlife watching and photography on almost all NWRs.

| Objective 3.2 – Provide Wildlife Observation and Photography Opportunities | |
|---|---|
| *Code* | *Strategy* |
| **Wildlife Observation and Photography** | |
| 3.2.1 | By 2005, design and install an orientation kiosk at the Refuge entrance that includes three signs: a sign providing a trail map, trail information, and trail regulations; a sign that describes the National Wildlife Refuge System and allowed uses on the Refuge; and interchangeable signs for hunting and snowy plover nesting seasons. |
| 3.2.2 | By 2007, construct and maintain a 1,500-foot trail accessible to persons with disabilities from the parking lot of the Refuge to the Salinas River. This trail would improve access to the river and to minimize the impacts of public use through these sensitive habitats (Figure 5). |
| 3.2.3 | By 2007, improve the parking lot with a gravel or other unpaved surface to provide visitors with better all-season parking at the Refuge. |
| 3.2.4 | Maintain trails on the Refuge and clearly delineate trail portion along the Salinas River. |
| 3.2.5 | Coordinate with the CCC and the Service's Endangered Species Division on the prospect of routing the proposed pedestrian Coastal Trail through the Refuge. Siting, design, and use of the trail would consider potential effects on sensitive resources and would need to be compatible with the Refuge's purpose. |

*Objective 3.3:*
*The Refuge will expand opportunities for interpretation and environmental education that will foster visitors' appreciation, understanding, and stewardship of the Refuge's habitats and protected species.*

Rationale: The Improvement Act identifies environmental interpretation and environmental education as priority uses on NWRs. Because these uses are often compatible with other refuge management goals, the Service actively encourages environmental education and interpretation on many refuges. The mission of the National Wildlife Refuge System encourages study sites, facilities, and active support for educational programs that focus on fish and wildlife resources and environmental problems. High-quality interpretive and educational opportunities will greatly enhance visitors' experience of the Refuge. Increased knowledge of Refuge resources will ensure a more comprehensive understanding of NWRs and their significance.

In addition, formal cultural resource surveys are highly recommended for the Refuge to complement ongoing and proposed biological and hydrologic studies; little information now exists on the Refuge's cultural resources, but activities included under all of the management alternatives have the potential to affect cultural resources. At a minimum, cultural resources inventories will be required in areas where ground-disturbing activities are proposed, including the use of prescribed fire and construction of trails or other facilities. In addition, the World War II bomb shelter should be formally recorded by a qualified cultural resources specialist.

Inventories, evaluation, or data recovery on cultural resources on the Refuge could help address important academic questions for the region. Any information gathered during cultural resource surveys will be incorporated into interpretive and educational material.

**Salinas River NWR CCP Planning Team on field visit**
*USFWS Photo*

| Objective 3.3 – Provide Interpretation and Education | |
|---|---|
| *Code* | *Strategy* |
| Interpretation and Education | |
| 3.3.1 | By 2007, design and install interpretive signs along existing trails to explain the ecology of native habitats on the Refuge and the species within them. |
| 3.3.2 | Maintain and enhance existing environmental education partnerships with the California State University and develop new partnerships with other local agencies, schools, universities, and organizations. |
| 3.3.3 | Develop environmental education and interpretive materials including a Refuge brochure, fact sheets on specific species and habitats, and a guide for educators on endangered species issues. |
| 3.3.4 | Conduct a sitewide inventory of potential archaeological and historic resources on the Refuge; incorporate information about these resources into interpretive and educational material (Strategies 3.3.1 and 3.3.3). |

Note: Strategies 2.2.5 and 2.2.6 also help to achieve this Objective.

*Objective 3.4:*
*The Refuge will take measures to ensure the safety of resources, property, and visitors.*

Rationale: Increased safety measures would enable the Refuge to better fulfill its conservation mission, and would ensure improved experiences for Refuge visitors.

| Objective 3.4 – Ensure Safety of Resources, Property, and Visitors | |
|---|---|
| *Code* | *Strategy* |
| Increase Safety Measures | |
| 3.4.1 | Increase law enforcement patrols. |
| 3.4.2 | Develop cooperative agreements with State and local agencies to support increased law enforcement patrols. |

## Mitigation Measures

Mitigation measures developed during the planning and environmental review processes have been incorporated into this CCP. Moreover, measures set forth in the *Biological Opinion for the Salinas River National Wildlife Refuge Comprehensive Conservation Plan, Monterey County, California* (U.S. Fish and Wildlife Service 2002) have also been incorporated. These measures are listed below by resource area. For additional information regarding the impacts addressed by these measures, the reader is directed to the draft CCP/EA (U.S. Fish and Wildlife Service 2001.)

*Water Quality/Contaminants*
Herbicides will be applied at label rates and all label recommendations will be followed. In addition, the following specific precautions will be taken to avoid and minimize impacts related to use of herbicides.
■ Herbicides will be selected based on the characteristics of each treatment site, including its location relative to aquatic and wetland habitats. (Existing management practice is to use Roundup™ at sites >100 feet from open water or wetlands and Rodeo™ at sites within 100 feet of open water or wetlands.)
■ No spraying will take place when wind velocities exceed 5 mph, when vegetation is wet, or when precipitation is occurring or is forecast in the following 24–36 hours. Wind meters and smoke devices will be used to assess wind direction and wind speed; smoke from existing burning

activity or smokestacks (such as those at Moss Landing) may be used to check for the presence of inversion conditions, if the source of smoke is near the application site and is similar in elevation to the application site.

- Nozzles with orifice diameters $\geq$1/16 inch, or low-drift flat spray nozzles, will be used. When appropriate, the lowest possible pressure within the nozzle's ideal range will be used.
- No spraying will occur if western snowy plovers are within 75 meters of the application site. No spraying will occur until all western snowy plover activity within 75 meters of the area to be treated has ceased for 7 days. Refuge staff will consult with Point Reyes Bird Observatory who are monitoring plovers on the Refuge to ensure that the species is absent from the work area.
- No spraying will occur in areas where endangered plants or host plants for Smith's blue butterfly may be affected by drift. Invasive non-natives in these areas will be mechanically removed.

### Hazardous Materials and Safety Issues

Closed area signs posted in the northwest corner of the Refuge will incorporate a warning about the low risk of encountering unexploded ordnance from past military activities.

### Biological Resources

Vegetation. The Service will maintain a trail through the grassland to the hunt area and will install and maintain signs marking the hunt area boundary. In addition, by 2007, interpretive signs and an orientation kiosk will be installed on the Refuge to inform visitors about the Refuge's habitats and wildlife and ways of avoiding adverse impacts, including staying on trails. The trails and interpretive signs will minimize disturbance to grassland and riparian habitats by providing easy access to the hunt area and by interpreting the importance and sensitivity of Refuge habitats and restoration efforts. Similarly, the trail to the beach will have symbolic cable fencing and interpretive signs. If necessary, cable fence will be installed along the foredune boundary (along the beach) as well.

Wildlife. The Service will maintain a trail through the grassland to the hunt area and will install and maintain signs marking the hunt area boundary. In addition, by 2007, interpretive signs and an orientation kiosk will be installed on the Refuge to inform visitors about the Refuge's habitats and wildlife and ways of avoiding adverse impacts, including staying on trails. The trails and interpretive signs will minimize disturbance to wildlife in upland, riparian, and aquatic habitats by providing easy access to the hunt area and by interpreting the importance and sensitivity of Refuge habitats and restoration efforts.

Interpretive signage, including the kiosk, will stress the need to avoid littering on the Refuge.

Hunters will be permitted to have no more than 25 shells in their possession while on the Refuge. This will discourage hunters from taking long shots, reducing noise-related disturbance of wildlife and decreasing the possibility of target misidentification and take of non-target species. Waterfowl hunters will be required to use only approved nontoxic shots while on the Refuge.

The Biological Opinion imposes a series of measures for addressing impacts, including take, that could affect western snowy plover, brown pelican, and Smith's blue butterfly.

Incidental Take. The Refuge will contact the Service whenever a dead western snowy plover or abandoned nest, a dead brown pelican, or a dead Smith's blue butterfly is found and the cause of death or injury is unknown or may be due to the Refuge's activities. Provided that protective measures proposed by the Refuge and the terms and conditions of the BO are being fully implemented, operations need not cease while the cause of mortality is being determined. Once the cause of death or injury has been determined, the Service shall decide, in cooperation with the Refuge, whether any additional protective measures are required to address the cause of the loss of the western snowy plover or nest, brown pelican, or Smith's blue butterfly.

Reasonable and Prudent Measures.
1.  Only qualified biologists shall monitor the status of the western snowy plover, brown pelican, and Smith's blue butterfly on the Refuge or monitor the installation or maintenance of symbolic fencing within western snowy plover nesting habitat during the breeding season.

2.  The Refuge shall use well-defined operational procedures, education programs, and qualified personnel to minimize the incidental take of western snowy plovers, brown pelicans, and Smith's blue butterflies during resource management and public use actions at the Refuge.

3.  The Refuge shall ensure that fencing or signs do not promote avian predator presence on the Refuge.

Terms and Conditions.
1.  The following term and condition implements reasonable and prudent measure 1:
    a.  Only qualified biologists covered under a section 10(a)(1)(A) recovery permit or approved by the Ventura Fish and Wildlife Office shall monitor the status of the western snowy plover, brown pelican, and Smith's blue butterfly on the Refuge or monitor the installation and maintenance of symbolic fencing within western snowy plover nesting habitat during the breeding season. The Refuge shall submit the credentials of individuals it wishes to conduct these activities to the Ventura Fish and Wildlife Office for review and approval at least 15 days prior to the onset of these activities. Once the Service has approved an individual to conduct these activities, this person may direct nonapproved individuals in these activities while on site.

2.  The following terms and conditions implement reasonable and prudent measure 2:
    a.  The Refuge shall instruct Refuge personnel and contractors on how best to conduct activities and reduce impacts on the listed species present on the Refuge before carrying out resource management and public use actions.

b. The Refuge shall train volunteer docents to identify all the listed species and their habitat on the Refuge, including western snowy plover nests, chicks, and eggs, to minimize the risk of crushing any that may be outside of exclosures. In addition, volunteer docents shall not be allowed to enter nesting areas unless properly trained and permitted to do so.

3. The following terms and conditions implement reasonable and prudent measure 3:
   a. The Refuge shall modify signs and fencing with anti-perching material to discourage perching if avian predators are determined to be frequenting them.

Disposition of Dead or Injured Specimens. Upon locating a dead or injured brown pelican, western snowy plover, or Smith's blue butterfly, initial notification must be made in writing to the Service's Division of Law Enforcement in Torrance, California (370 Amapola Avenue, Suite 114, Torrance, CA 90501) and by telephone and writing to the Ventura Fish and Wildlife Office in Ventura, California (2493 Portola Road, Suite B, Ventura, CA 93003, [805] 644-1766) within 3 working days of the finding. The report shall include the date, time, location of the carcass, a photograph, cause of death, if known, and any other pertinent information.

Care shall be taken in handling dead specimens to preserve biological material in the best possible state for later analysis. Should any injured birds survive, the Service should be contacted regarding their final disposition. The remains of intact brown pelicans, western snowy plovers, and Smith's blue butterflies shall be placed with the California Academy of Sciences, Golden Gate Park, San Francisco, California; or the Museum of Vertebrate Zoology, University of California, Berkeley, California.

In the case of take or suspected take of listed species not exempted in the BO, the Ventura Fish and Wildlife Office shall be notified within 24 hours.

Reporting Requirement. The Refuge shall provide a written annual report to the Ventura Fish and Wildlife Office within 90 days following the end of each year that this BO is in effect. The report shall document the number of western snowy plovers, brown pelicans, and Smith's blue butterflies killed or injured by the proposed activities. The report shall also include a quantification of dune habitat (including numbers of Monterey gilia, Monterey spineflower, and Smith's blue butterfly host plants) disturbed or degraded by human disturbance or the spread of invasive nonnative vegetation. The report shall also contain a discussion of activities that resulted in disturbance to nesting western snowy plovers and brown pelicans; the results of biological surveys and sighting records; the results of management activities carried out on the Refuge; and any other pertinent information. This document will assist the Ventura Fish and Wildlife Office and the Refuge in evaluating future measures for the conservation of the species during ongoing activities and for future projects.

## *Cultural Resources*

All undertakings, including but not limited to ground-disturbing activities and prescribed burns, will be coordinated with the Service's Regional Archaeologist, in order to preserve the Refuge's archaeologic and historic resources of the Refuge. Following are specific guidelines that may apply, depending on site-specific conditions.

- A cultural resources survey by a qualified archaeologist may be required in areas where a ground-disturbing activity or prescribed burning is proposed. If burning is proposed entirely within a flood zone or in a previously disked or plowed area, or if burning has been an ongoing practice on the site, a cultural resources survey may not be required. However, cultural resources surveys will likely be necessary for all burns on upland sites, and for burns that require excavation (scraping, plowing, or disking) to establish a fireline. In some cases, it may be appropriate to conduct cultural resources survey work after a prescribed burn has been completed, because (1) visibility of artifacts or other resources may be increased after burning, and (2) artifacts may be more vulnerable to vandalism or theft when exposed by burning.

- As required by the Native American Graves Protection and Repatriation Act (NAGPRA) (25 USC 3001 et seq. or 43 CFR 10), any construction or ground-disturbing activity on the Refuge with the potential to disturb human remains, burial objects, sacred objects, or objects of cultural patrimony will be planned and implemented in consultation with affected Tribes.

- If potentially significant artifacts are found during any activity on the Refuge, work will cease within 100 feet of the find and access will be restricted until a qualified archaeologist and members of local Tribes can assess the significance of the find and propose appropriate methods of treatment, as required by NAGPRA.

- If human remains are found during any activity on the Refuge, work will cease within 100 feet of the find and access will be restricted, and the Monterey County Coroner will been informed of the discovery, under Public Resources Code Section 5050.5. If no investigation of the cause of death is required, remains will be treated in accordance with the requirements of NAGPRA.

# Chapter 4. Existing Conditions

This chapter describes the characteristics and resources of the Refuge. It specifically addresses physical resources, biological resources, cultural resources, socioeconomic resources, and recreational opportunities.

## Physical Resources

### Climate

Like the rest of the California coast, northwestern Monterey County enjoys a Mediterranean climate, with dry, warm summers and moderately wet, mild winters. Precipitation in the Refuge area averages approximately 16 inches per year, 90% of which falls between November and April (Soil Conservation Service 1978). Prevailing winds throughout most of the year are northwesterly. During the late summer and fall, prevailing winds are southeasterly.

### Surface Hydrology

The Refuge is located at the western (downstream) end of the Salinas River watershed. This watershed, between the Santa Lucia and Diablo ranges, is approximately 150 miles long and averages 20–40 miles wide. It is one of the larger watersheds in California, draining an area of 4,231 square miles.

**Saline pond on Salinas River NWR**
*USFWS Photo*

Surface drainage in the vicinity of the Refuge is dominated by the gradients associated with the Salinas River and the Pacific Ocean. Much of the surface runoff in the project area drains in a general northward direction into the Salinas River. Some runoff may also drain west, directly into the Pacific Ocean, via overland flow or via subsurface flow under the dune lands. In addition to natural runoff, off-site drainage from agricultural lands south of the project site is conveyed northward into the Refuge. Agricultural runoff apparently flows into the Refuge's large saline pond; if the capacity of the saline pond is exceeded, runoff overflows northward into the Salinas River.

The Refuge's saline pond is likely a remnant of an abandoned meander of the Salinas River. Based on analysis of historic U.S. Coast and Geodetic Survey maps, the pond has existed since at least 1857 (John Gilchrist & Associates et al. 1997) and was connected to the Salinas River until 1913. Since its formation, the pond has gradually shrunk in size and depth, probably in part because of gradual infiltration and in part because of encroachment by the Refuge's eastward- migrating dunes. Nonetheless, this 15-acre pond and associated salt marsh are noteworthy, as there are few other saline ponds of this type on the central California coast.

In addition to agricultural runoff, the Refuge's saline pond also receives input from rainfall, from seawater that washes over the dunes, from groundwater, and, during major floods, from the Salinas River. The depth of the pond varies in response to the balance among these factors. Between 1989 and 1991, the depth of the pond ranged from 0.5 foot to 2.0 feet; the pond was nearly dry in November 1990. As water levels drop, salt from seawater input concentrates in the pond. Water salinity in the pond ranges from 1 part per thousand (ppt) immediately after heavy rains to 150 ppt during prolonged droughts; for comparison, the salinity of seawater is about 35 ppt.

The Salinas River. Like all rivers, the Salinas River is a dynamic system. Under natural conditions, its course changes because of gradual, ongoing processes of erosion and sediment deposition. During major floods, these processes may be accelerated, resulting in rapid shifts in the location of the active river channel.

Historic maps of the Salinas area show that the course of the Salinas River has altered significantly over the past two centuries (John Gilchrist & Associates et al. 1997). In 1857, the river entered what is now the Refuge from the northeast rather than the southeast. By 1933 the river occupied a channel similar in location and configuration to its present course, which describes a gentle northwestward curve across the Refuge. Since at least the 1930s, the south bank of the river (the outside of the curve) has slowly eroded, while the north bank (the inside of the curve) has built southward through the steady accumulation of sediment. Thus, the Salinas River channel has shifted to the southwest, farther onto the Refuge site; the net result has been to reduce the amount of land and increase the amount of open water within the Refuge boundary. This natural process of channel migration is expected to continue for the foreseeable future.

In an attempt to slow the rate of erosion along the Salinas River's south bank, erosion-control structures were installed along the river near the Highway 1 bridge immediately upstream from the Refuge. Some of the structures have failed and been washed away; others have succeeded in slowing erosion locally. The width of the stabilized reach of the channel has decreased from ~600 feet in 1933 to ~150 feet today, in part because the stabilized south bank is prevented from migrating laterally while sediment deposition continues on the north bank (John Gilchrist & Associates et al. 1997). Flow diversions may also have contributed to the decrease in channel width.

On the Refuge, the Salinas River's south bank is unprotected and experiences significant erosion. One goal of riparian restoration work along the south bank of the river in the Refuge is to slow the rate of bank erosion. The *Biological Resources* section of this chapter contains additional information on riparian restoration on the Refuge.

**Riparian restoration along Salinas River**
*Jones & Stokes Photo*

Flooding:
The central California coast, including the Refuge, experiences annual flooding related to winter storms originating over the Pacific Ocean. Extended periods of heavy rainfall produce floods characterized by a rapid rise in streamflow. The subsequent decrease in streamflow may be almost as rapid; however, a series of storms, or a single stalled stormfront, can produce large, catastrophic riverine floods. Flooding in the coastal areas of Monterey County is also associated with simultaneous occurrence of very high tides and large waves. Property damage results from erosion, flotation, and inundation, and from the deposition of debris on downstream properties.

The Federal Emergency Management Agency's Flood Insurance Rate Maps indicate that, except for the coastal dunes and the upper terrace deposits along the site's southern boundary, much of the Refuge is within the 100-year floodplain of the Salinas River. This means that under natural conditions much of the Refuge should be inundated every 100 years on the average. The 100-year water surface elevation ranges from 8.8 feet above mean sea level near the mouth of the Salinas River to 10.6 feet above mean sea level at the eastern boundary of the Refuge (Federal Emergency Management Agency 1991).

Lagoon Breaching:
The mouth of the Salinas River experiences intermittent partial blockage as a result of natural sandbar development. This causes water levels in the Salinas River Lagoon behind the bar to rise; agricultural lands to the north of the Salinas River begin to flood when the stage in the lagoon exceeds approximately 5.5 feet. To prevent flooding, the Monterey County Water Resources Agency (MCWRA) periodically breaches the sandbar in the winter from the north side of the Salinas River Lagoon through adjacent State property according to the Salinas River Lagoon Management and Enhancement Plan. (John Gilchrist & Associates et al. 1997.) Though this activity occurs on State-owned lands, the Refuge does coordinate with the MCWRA and is a member of the Salinas River Lagoon Task Force.

MCWRA breaches the rivermouth under the following conditions:
- When flows of approximately 500 cfs or greater are forecast at the U.S. Geological Survey gage at Spreckles;
- When forecast extended flows might cause flooding on nearby farmland if the Salinas River mouth is not breached;
- When the water level in the Salinas River Lagoon is high, and continuous or imminent river flow into the lagoon is forecast; or
- When a forecast by the MCWRA's ALERT flood warning system indicates that flow into the Salinas River Lagoon will result in flooding if the rivermouth is not breached.

It takes approximately 24–48 hours to mobilize and clear a channel through the sandbar with a bulldozer (John Gilchrist & Associates et al. 1997). The timing of breaching affects both water level and water salinity in the lagoon.

Water Quality. Water quality in the Salinas River has been altered by a number of practices, including:
- Surface-water diversion,
- Groundwater pumping,
- Diking and drainage of wetlands,
- Agriculture, and
- Contamination from industrial point sources and from urban runoff.

Alteration of flows alters the salt balance in the Salinas River Lagoon and adjacent marshes, but the greatest threats to water quality in the lagoon and the saline pond on the Refuge are nutrients and pesticides from adjacent and upstream agricultural lands. At present, it is unknown whether the Refuge receives these contaminants from agricultural runoff. Excess nutrients may cause eutrophication, or over-enrichment in nutrients, producing excess growth of algae and mortality of other organisms; this in turn decreases concentrations of dissolved oxygen and contributes to noxious odors. Persistent pesticides in the area may include DDT, toxaphene, dieldrin, endrin, aldrin, and endosulfan, all of which have been used extensively in the Salinas Valley. The use of these pesticides has been banned in California, but they were used for many years, and are known to have been used extensively in the Salinas Valley (John Gilchrist & Associates et al. 1997). These pesticides have been linked to various problems in local wildlife, including widespread mortality resulting from spills, reproductive failure caused by bioaccumulation, behavioral and physiological problems, decreased food consumption, and increased susceptibility to predation and cold.

### Geology

Geologic Setting. The Refuge is located in a portion of the California Coast Ranges referred to as Salinia or the Salinian block. Basement rocks in the Coast Ranges are as old as Mesozoic (65–245 million years old) (e.g., Jennings and Strand 1959), and record the long and complex history of the California continental margin. However, the Coast Range itself is a relatively recent feature. Uplift of the Coast Range probably began no earlier than about 5–8 million years ago (Buising and Walker 1995, Atwater and Stock 1998), and uplift of some parts of the range has continued into the past 2 million years (Burgmann et al. 1994, Sedlock 1995). The region is also currently experiencing active strike-slip tectonics related to the San Andreas fault system.

The Salinian block, bounded on the landward side by the San Andreas fault, and on the oceanward side by the offshore San Gregorio-Hosgri fault system, is a geologic orphan, sliced off of rocks to the south and slid into its current location by large-scale translation along the San Andreas fault (Mattinson and James 1985). Unlike adjacent portions of the Coast Ranges, which are largely underlain by basement rocks belonging to the Franciscan complex, Salinia is characterized by a basement assemblage of plutonic (granitic-granodioritic) and metamorphic rock (e.g., Mattinson and James 1985). In the vicinity of the Refuge, this crystalline basement is overlain by terrestrial and marine sedimentary strata that range from Miocene to Pliocene (approximately 23 million years to 1.6 million years) in age. The Refuge itself is situated primarily on inactive dune deposits of Pleistocene age (1.6 million to approximately 10,000 years old), on active coastal deposits (including active dunes) and on active alluvium of the Salinas River floodplain (see Jennings and Strand 1959).

Seismic Activity. The Refuge is located in a seismically active region. Although the Refuge does not encompass any active faults (defined by the California Division of Mines and Geology as faults that have experienced motion in the last 11,000 years) (Hart and Bryant 1997), the San Andreas fault zone is located less than 15 miles northeast of the Refuge. Several strong earthquakes have occurred within a 50-mile radius of the Refuge. The closest recorded strong earthquake occurred in 1910, approximately 8 miles north of the Refuge; it measured 5.3 on the Richter scale (Ellsworth 1990). The 1989 Loma Prieta earthquake, with a Richter magnitude of 6.9, was epicentered approximately 20 miles northwest of the Refuge (http://www.quake.usgs.gov/prepare/ index.html, accessed June 16, 2001). Because of its proximity to active fault strands, the Refuge can be expected to experience ongoing earthquake activity in the future.

## Soils

Overview of Soils on the Refuge. Soils in the Refuge area include the following mapped units: Alviso silty clay loam, coastal beaches, Metz fine sandy loam, Mocho silty loam, Mocho silty clay loam, and Pico fine sandy loam (Soil Conservation Service 1978). Table 4 summarizes the characteristics of the Refuge's soil units.

Soils of the Refuge include floodplain and tidal basin soils, as well as a substantial area of coastal dunes. The Refuge's dune lands represent the northern tip of a dune system that extends more than 12 miles south of the Refuge, reflecting the combined influences of the Salinas River, coastal waves and tides, and prevailing winds. Sand is supplied primarily by longshore transport of sediment delivered by rivers to the north (including the Salinas River) and is reworked and sculpted into dune forms largely by onshore winds. High storm tides subject the dunes to intermittent wave erosion.

The Refuge's dune system is highly dynamic, shifting its position and form in response to changes in the balance between sand supply, wind transport, and wave erosion. Analysis of historic maps shows that between 1937 and 1987, the beach and dunes on the Refuge migrated landward approximately 300–400 feet to cover approximately 13 acres of the salt marsh and the saline pond. This change is equivalent to an average of 6–10 feet of landward migration per year. This rate of movement is not unique to the Refuge; similar rates have been measured in the dunes and beaches in nearby Marina, Seaside, and Monterey (John Gilchrist & Associates et al. 1997).

**Central dune scrub habitat on Salinas River NWR**
*Jones & Stokes Photo*

**Table 4. Soils of the Salinas River National Wildlife Refuge.**

| Soil Unit | Description | Permeability/Runoff | Erosion Hazard | Depth to Water Table |
|---|---|---|---|---|
| Alviso silty clay loam | Typically <20 inches thick; occurs in basins and on tidal flats. | Low/Very Slow (Very poorly drained under natural conditions.) | Low | 6 12 inches |
| Coastal beaches | Characterized by a narrow sandy strand and adjacent sand dunes; partly inundated during high tide and exposed during low tide. May consist of sand, gravel, and cobbles, in any combination. | Very Rapid/Very Slow | Very High | |
| Dune lands | Gently sloping to steep landforms composed of loose, wind deposited quartz and feldspar sands. | Very Rapid/Very Slow | Very High (subject to wind erosion) | |
| Metz fine sandy loam | Nearly level floodplain deposit. | Moderate/Slow | Slight, but subject to effects of wind | Typically > 60 inches |
| Mocho silty loam | Formed on floodplains in alluvium derived primarily from sedimentary rocks. | Moderate/Slow | Slight | Typically > 60 inches |
| Mocho silty clay loam | Formed on floodplains in alluvium derived primarily from sedimentary rocks. | Slow/Slow | Slight | Typically > 60 inches |
| Pico fine sandy loam | Formed on floodplains in alluvium derived primarily from sedimentary rocks. | Moderately Rapid/Slow | Slight, but subject to effects of wind | Typically > 60 inches |

Source: Soil Conservation Service 1978

<u>Soils-Related Hazards on the Refuge.</u> The following paragraphs briefly discuss soils-related hazards that may affect land use decisions on the Refuge.

*Expansive soils* contain clay minerals (the so-called "swelling clays") that take on water and expand when wetted and contract again as they dry. Structures built on expansive soils—for example, buildings, pavements, and embankments—may be damaged by the movement and settlement that accompany this shrink-swell behavior. At the Refuge, the Alviso,

Mocho, and Pico soils exhibit moderate to high shrink-swell potential; the area's other soils have low shrink-swell potential (Soil Conservation Service 1978).

*Erosive soils* are soils that are particularly vulnerable to erosion by water, typically because of loose textures (low clay content) and/or steep slopes. Excessive erosion generally occurs when human intervention accelerates the natural erosion process. Removal of vegetation and decrease in permeable surface area, both of which are common corollaries of development, can increase surface runoff, which may in turn increase erosion rates. Increased erosion generally causes increased sediment loading in area creeks and rivers, and may result in gullying that undermines remaining vegetation. Some of the Refuge's soils occur on steep slopes or have loose textures, and as a result exhibit moderate to high erosion potential. In addition, the Refuge's coastal beaches, dune lands, and sandy soils are subject to wind erosion.

*Corrosive soils* are soils whose chemistry is such that they may react with and damage a variety of construction materials when wet. Corrosivity of soils to steel is related to soil moisture, total acidity, and electrical conductivity of the soil; corrosivity of soils to concrete is related to the sulfate content and acidity of the soil. Unless precautions are taken, corrosive soils can eventually cause foundation and structural damage. In the Refuge area, Alviso soils are typically highly corrosive to uncoated steel and concrete and Metz, Mocho, and Pico soils are corrosive to uncoated steel (Soil Conservation Service 1978).

### Air Quality

The Refuge is located in California's North-Central Coast Air Basin (NCCAB). The NCCAB is subject to State and Federal air quality standards. Areas that do not meet the standards are designated as nonattainment areas, and those that do comply are designated as attainment areas.

The primary types of pollutants regulated by State and Federal law include:
- Particulate matter less than 10 microns in diameter (PM10),
- Ozone,
- Carbon monoxide (CO),
- Oxides of nitrogen ($NO_x$),
- Sulfur dioxide ($SO_2$), and
- Lead.

The NCCAB is an attainment area for both State and Federal CO, $NO_x$, $SO_2$, and lead ambient standards, and for Federal PM10 and ozone standards. It is a nonattainment area for State PM10 and ozone ambient standards.

The Monterey Bay Unified Air Pollution Control District (Air District) is the local agency responsible for ensuring compliance with State and Federal air quality standards in the Refuge area (see California Air Resources Board website, http://www.arb.ca.gov/homepage.htm). It is unlikely that Refuge operations would affect ozone levels. However, Refuge management activities that alter the area's hydrology or vegetative cover may expose soil to blowing wind, possibly increasing PM10 emissions.

*Hazardous Materials and Contaminants*

Because of both past and current land uses, hazardous materials or contaminants may be present on the Refuge. Potential sources of hazardous materials or contaminants include the Refuge's past military use, past and current agricultural operations, and current mosquito control operations.

Military Use. Between 1942 and 1973, the U.S. military operated several facilities on what are now Refuge lands (see *United States Military at the Refuge* in *Cultural Resources* below for a summary of the Refuge's military history). As discussed below, the exact nature of these operations is unknown. However, when lands that now make up the Refuge were transferred from the Army to the Service, the Army removed several small facilities built in 1945 during the Navy's tenure, including a power substation, a garage, a bomb shelter, and aboveground features associated with two water wells (185 and 196 feet deep, respectively). Records of the removal of these structures provide some indication of the site's former land uses and give some suggestion of the types of contaminants or hazardous materials that may remain on the Refuge as a result of former military operations. Additionally, the Department of Defense recently assessed the potential for contamination on the Refuge under the Defense Environmental Restoration Program (DERP) (U.S. Army Corps of Engineers 1999). Their assessment consisted of a review of the site's history, interviews with individuals familiar with the site and its history, and a site visit to perform random visual search and a metal detector survey.

Records show that the Army had an officers' hunting club at the Refuge site. This may have resulted in some level of lead contamination, but the current concentration of lead in the site's soils and in the sediments of the Salinas River Lagoon is unknown.

Part of what is now the Refuge was used by the Navy for aerial bombing practice. The target was a 550-foot long and 65-foot wide silhouette of a cruiser located behind the active dunes in the northwestern corner of the Refuge. Records indicate that the bombs used contained small spotting charges rather than explosives. In addition, other sites in the vicinity of the Refuge were used for shore bombardment practice by Navy ships; however, the Refuge lands were not used for that purpose. Since the establishment of the Refuge, there has been only one incident of anyone finding live ordnance. This occurred in late 1997 when a visitor found a live 5-inch Navy projectile on the beach. The explosive was detonated on-site by an expert from Moffett Field. Because the Refuge was not used for shore bombardment, the projectile likely washed ashore in the past and was uncovered by the tides. The random visual and metal detector survey conducted by the U.S. Army Corps of Engineers in 1998 did not detect any further ordnance, spent or live, on the Refuge (U.S. Army Corps of Engineers 1999). A second site visit was conducted by the Corps on June 6, 2001 to investigate the potential for unexploded ordnance or other hazardous material on the Refuge; none was found.

The U.S. Army Corps of Engineers uses two measures to prioritize further investigation and remediation of former defense sites: hazard severity and hazard probability. Based on their historic investigation, interviews, and site visit, the Corps gave the Refuge a hazard severity value of 6 on a scale of 0 (lowest severity) to 60 (highest severity), which represents "marginal severity." The site was given a hazard probability value of 13 on a scale of 0 (lowest probability) to 30 (highest probability). Overall, the site was given a risk assessment code of 4, which is the lowest code that corresponds to a recommendation for action by the Corps (U.S. Army Corps of Engineers 1999). The June 2001 site visit confirmed the very low probability of hazards on the Refuge. The Refuge may be investigated further by the Corps, but in view of the low risk rating and resulting low priority, it may be many years before this investigation is conducted. The former target range is already closed to the public to protect sensitive habitats.

In 1992, a 3,000-gallon underground storage tank was discovered in the southeast corner of the Refuge, approximately 500 feet from the Salinas River and less than one mile from the Pacific Ocean. The tank contained a mixture of diesel fuel and water that had leaked in over time. The tank, an associated pipeline, and the surrounding soil were subsequently removed from the site in June 1997. As part of this remediation, 250 cubic yards of soil were cleaned and spread on the site and 13,300 gallons of groundwater were pumped out of the area and taken to an off-site disposal facility (Regional Water Quality Control Board 1998, U.S. Army Corps of Engineers 1999). The excavation site was backfilled with clean soil. The Monterey County Department of Health confirmed the completion of site remediation and site closure in a letter dated February 12, 1999.

Agriculture. Past and current agricultural use in the area is also a potential source of contamination on the Refuge. Prior to 1973, part of the Refuge was in agricultural production. The Refuge receives runoff from agricultural areas to the south and across the Salinas River to the north. As a result, the saline pond and Salinas Lagoon are probably intermittently contaminated by pesticides and nutrients from upstream agricultural lands. In addition, because the Refuge is located at the downstream end of the highly agricultural Salinas River Valley, the finer-textured soils on the Refuge may contain persistent pesticides such as DDT, toxaphene, dieldrin, endrin, aldrin, and endosulfan (now banned in California).

After heavy flooding in 1995, an area along the Salinas River was exposed and found to contain debris and waste that may have been a former small landfill (U.S. Army Corps of Engineers 1999). The origins of this site are unknown but it may have been established during agricultural operations on the Refuge prior to 1973. There are no records of an active landfill in the records of military use of the Refuge. The possible landfill site has not been observed in the years since 1995, possibly because the debris has washed into the Salinas Lagoon.

Mosquito Control. The Northern Salinas Valley Mosquito Abatement District (NSVMAD) has been conducting mosquito control at the Refuge for many years. Chemical spraying is conducted almost exclusively by helicopter. On rare occasions, when the treatment area is small, spraying is done by hand. Aerial applications are made from an altitude of 5–10 feet at an airspeed of 55 mph. Swath width is 66 feet, so several passes are made. Treatment duration is approximately 15–20 minutes.

Mosquito populations are related to precipitation amounts. In years when rainfall is below normal, mosquito populations are low and control is reduced or nonexistent. Conversely, when rainfall is above normal, mosquito populations are larger and mosquito control is increased. In the last six years, mosquito control applications occurred approximately 2–4 times per year. Spraying typically occurs from December through April in the saline pond and salt marsh habitat on the Refuge.

Since 1996, NSVMAD has used either VectoBac© G or 12AS to treat all or most of the Refuge. BothVectoBac© G and 12AS are aqueous suspensions of *Bacillus thuringiensis,* an insecticidal bacterium. The strain used by NSVMAD specifically targets mosquitoes, black flies, and fungus gnats and is non-toxic to humans, wildlife, and plants (National Integrated Pest Management Network, http://www.colostate.edu/Depts/IPM/, accessed June 2001). Two other chemicals could be used by NSVMAD to increase effectiveness: Golden Bear 1111, a petroleum distillate, and Altosid ALL, otherwise known as S-methoprene. Material selection is based on efficacy, mosquito instar present, water temperature, and species of mosquito.

Currently, NSVMAD does not have a Special Use Permit from the Service. Typically, they notify the Refuge 1–2 days before spraying. In the future, the Service will require a Special Use Permit each year that NSVMAD conducts spraying. This permit will stipulate that all control work will be carried out in conformance with pre-approved Pesticide Use Proposals and Section 7 Endangered Species consultations.

NSVMAD will notify the Refuge prior to monitoring or treating so that Refuge staff can determine whether treatment will be allowed based on the presence of nesting birds. The Refuge recognizes that a notification period of several days prior to treatment may allow larval development of mosquitos and precipitate the use of more harmful treatment materials (e.g., Golden Bear, a pupicidal oil). Therefore, NSVMAD will be required to notify the Refuge prior to monitoring/sampling efforts so Refuge staff will be aware that treatment may be imminent. In all cases, the permittee will give as much notice to the Refuge as is possible, and at least 24 hours notice. Spraying is not allowed during the shorebird nesting season (March 15–August 31) if avocets or stilts are known to be incubating or if snowy plovers with chicks are utilizing the pond. Terms and conditions of the Special Use Permit will be subject to annual modification if helicopter disturbance is considered to interfere with or detract from the fulfillment of the purpose of the Refuge. For more information on this activity, see Appendix G (*Compatibility Determinations*).

## Biological Resources at the Refuge
*Historic and Regional Context*
Historic accounts describe the Salinas Valley area as a rich patchwork of shallow lakes, sloughs, vernal pools, marsh vegetation, expanses of grassland, and riparian corridors. The Salinas River was part of a large wetland ecosystem that included Elkhorn Slough and the Pajaro River. This wetland once supported California grizzly bear, tule elk, and a great number and diversity of waterbirds.

Beginning with early European settlement in California, extensive areas were converted for agricultural purposes. By the early 1900s, much of the land in the lower Salinas Valley was under agricultural cultivation. A series of large finger lakes and associated wetlands had been drained, vernal pools were converted to cropland, and riparian habitat was removed. The Salinas and Pajaro Rivers were channelized and their wetlands drained, fragmenting the wetland ecosystem and reducing its size. The conversion of valuable wildlife habitat to cropland and pastures resulted in substantial adverse effects on the area's wildlife. The reduction in wetland area led to a significant drop in the numbers and diversity of the area's bird population (particularly waterbirds and neotropical migrant species), the extirpation of bear and tule elk from the region, and the probable loss of many vernal pool species.

More than 90% of the Salinas Valley's original wetlands have been converted to agricultural production. Lands that now make up the Refuge were spared from conversion because of their close proximity to the ocean, their susceptibility to flooding, and their former military ownership. The Refuge is now one of only a few places in the area where a significant expanse of wetland and riparian habitat remains.

Today, despite its small size, the Refuge supports some of the most important habitat for wildlife on the central California coast (John Gilchrist & Associates et al. 1997). Its importance reflects its unique wildlife and diversity of habitats, as well as the lack of remaining wetland habitat elsewhere on the central coast. The Refuge now plays a key role in protecting and sustaining wildlife resources, including the many migratory birds that follow the Pacific Flyway. The *Riparian Bird Conservation Plan* (Riparian Habitat Joint Venture 2000) recognizes the Salines River as a *Portfolio Site*, important because it contains the largest remaining riparian habitat in the central coast region of the state and historically supported least Bell's vireo, a species listed as endangered under the ESA. Moreover, the *Southern Pacific Coast Regional Shorebird Plan* (Page and Shuford 2000) identifies the Salinas River mouth as a wetland of importance to shorebirds, accommodating up to 1,000 shorebirds in fall and spring.

## Vegetation

The Refuge supports seven different types of natural plant communities that are typical of coastal dune, salt marsh, riparian, and disturbed environments on the central California coast (Figure 7).[1] The diversity of plant communities on the Refuge reflects variations in the site's soils, topography, and hydrology. Wetland plant communities are found along the Salinas River, Salinas River Lagoon, saline pond, and in low-lying areas in the central portion of the Refuge. Wetland communities include northern coastal salt marsh, coastal brackish marsh, and central coast riparian scrub. Upland plant communities are found at higher elevations in the Refuge. The Refuge's sand dune complex, which includes both active and stabilized dunes and consists of sands deposited by the Salinas River and redistributed by wind and wave action, provides the major topographic relief in the Refuge. The plant communities of the active dune and beach areas include central foredunes and central dune scrub. The dominant plant community in the Refuge is coyote brush scrub, which occupies stabilized dune uplands over most of the southern portion of the Refuge. Some of the plant species found on the Refuge are listed in Table C-1 in Appendix C.

---

[1]The vegetation classification used in this CCP is based on Holland (1986). A matrix correlating the Refuge's vegetation types with the National Vegetation Classification System (Federal Geographic Data Committee 1997) is presented in Appendix D.

<u>Vegetation in Wetland Areas</u>. Vegetation in the Refuge's wetland areas includes northern coastal salt marsh and coast brackish marsh, as well as freshwater riparian vegetation such as central coast arroyo willow riparian forest and central coast riparian scrub.

Northern Coastal Salt Marsh:
Northern coastal salt marsh is limited to areas with saturated soils and a narrow range of water salinities and water depths. This plant community is typically found at elevations between 0.75 and 2 m above mean sea level (msl) on the Refuge (John Gilchrist & Associates et al. 1997). Much of the central portion of the Refuge immediately inland from the sand dunes (as far north as the Salinas River Lagoon) supports northern coastal salt marsh vegetation. This community also occurs in small depressions within the coastal sand dune complex. Along the Salinas River, salt marsh habitat is replaced by coastal brackish marsh because of decreasing salinity.

The northern coastal salt marsh community is dominated by low-growing (<1 m high) perennial subshrubs that are tolerant of saturation, inundation, and high levels of salinity. The dominant species of northern coastal salt marsh are pickleweed (*Salicornia virginica*), alkali heath (*Frankenia grandiflora*), and fleshy jaumea (*Jaumea carnosa*). At slightly higher elevations mixed halophytes become dominant, including coastal gumplant (*Grindelia latifolia*), salt grass (*Distichlis spicata*) and alkali heath. The margins (typically the highest elevations) of the salt marshes support a grassland community dominated by salt grass, wet-meadow wild rye (*Leymus triticoides*), and Baltic rush (*Juncus balticus*) (John Gilchrist & Associates et al. 1997).

Coast Brackish Marsh:
Coast brackish marsh occurs in areas lower in elevation and more subject to regular flooding than those that support northern coastal salt marsh. On the Refuge, coast brackish marsh is most widespread at elevations of less than 0.75 m above msl along the Salinas River (John Gilchrist & Associates et al. 1997). Coast brackish marsh is dominated by perennial or annual herbaceous plants such as rabbitsfoot grass (*Polypogon monspeliensis*), threesquare (*Scirpus pungens*), alkali bulrush (*S. robustus*), California bulrush (*S. californicus*), and cattail (*Typha* spp.).

Central Coast Riparian Scrub:
Central coast riparian scrub typically forms a narrow band adjacent to an active stream channel. In some places it may represent an early successional stage that may, if left undisturbed over time, develop into a riparian forest. At the Refuge, central coast riparian scrub occurs along the Salinas River and on islands within the river. Dominant species in this plant community include willows such as arroyo willow (*Salix lasiolepis*), red willow (*S. laevigata*), sandbar willow (*S. hindsiana*), and yellow willow (*S. lasiandra*). The understory is typically dense and consists of young trees and shrubs such as poison oak (*Toxicodendron diversilobum*), Himalayan blackberry (*Rubus ursinus*), flowering currant (*Ribes sanguineum*), tree tobacco (*Nicotiana glauca*), mulefat (*Baccharis salicifolia*), coyote brush (*Baccharis pilularis*), mugwort (*Artemisia douglasiana*), and California rose (*Rosa californica*), as well as herbaceous plants such as fleshy jaumea, salt grass, and coastal gumplant (John Gilchrist & Associates et al. 1997).

# Figure 7. Vegetation Map

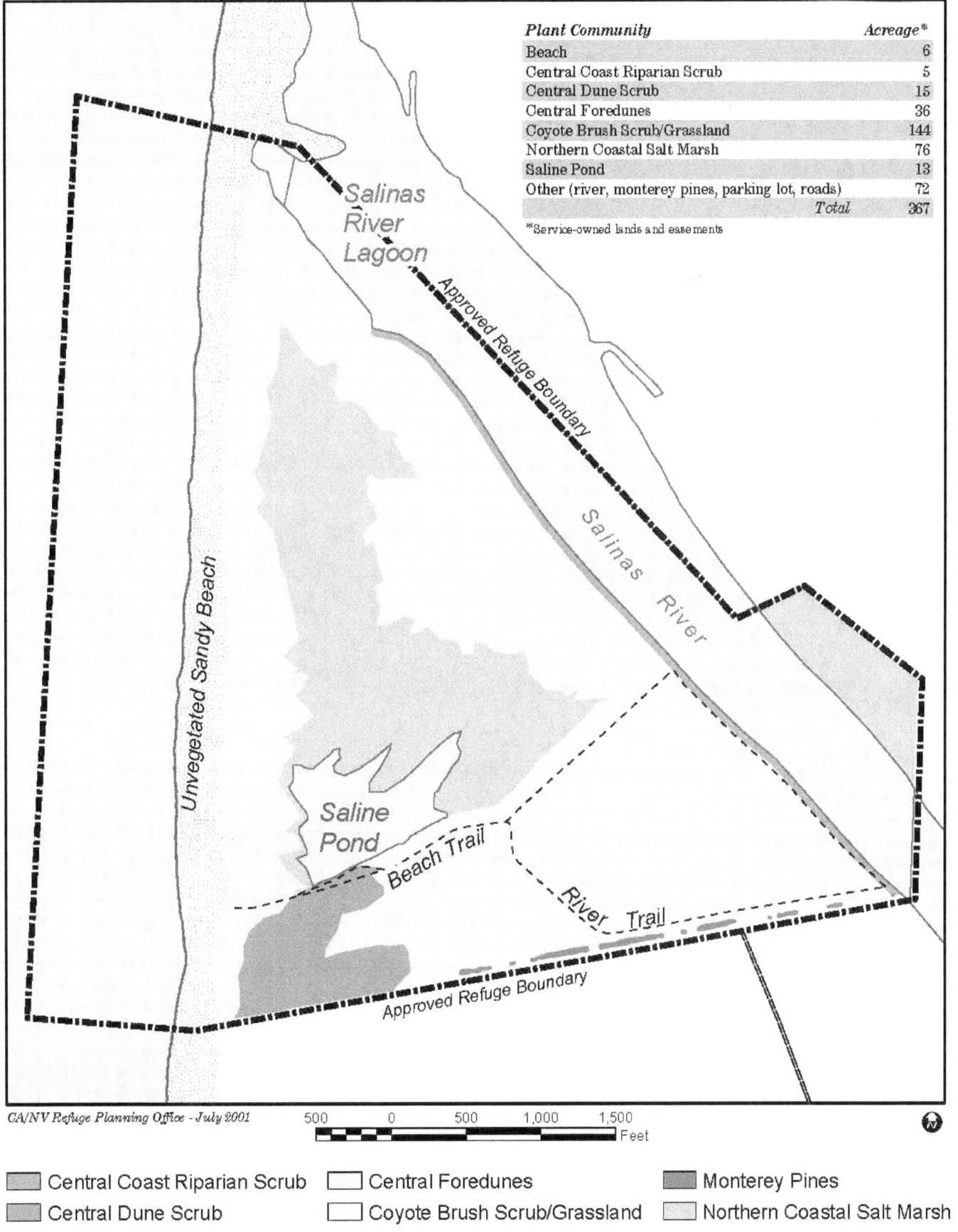

| Plant Community | Acreage* |
|---|---|
| Beach | 6 |
| Central Coast Riparian Scrub | 5 |
| Central Dune Scrub | 15 |
| Central Foredunes | 36 |
| Coyote Brush Scrub/Grassland | 144 |
| Northern Coastal Salt Marsh | 76 |
| Saline Pond | 13 |
| Other (river, monterey pines, parking lot, roads) | 72 |
| *Total* | 367 |

*Service-owned lands and easements

Salinas River Lagoon

Unvegetated Sandy Beach

Salinas River

Approved Refuge Boundary

Saline Pond

Beach Trail

River Trail

Approved Refuge Boundary

CA/NV Refuge Planning Office - July 2001

500   0   500   1,000   1,500 Feet

Central Coast Riparian Scrub   Central Foredunes   Monterey Pines

Central Dune Scrub   Coyote Brush Scrub/Grassland   Northern Coastal Salt Marsh

Researchers and students from the Watershed Institute of California State University, Monterey Bay are conducting intensive restoration activities along the banks of the Salinas River in an effort to reestablish native riparian scrub vegetation and to slow bank erosion. Species that have been planted along the bank include willows, box elder (*Acer negundo*), creekside dogwood (*Cornus sericea* ssp. *occidentalis*), red alder (*Alnus rubra*), and black cottonwood (*Populus trichocarpa*).

<u>Vegetation in Upland Areas</u>. Upland areas on the Refuge support three distinct types of plant communities. Central foredunes and central dune scrub communities are found on the Refuge's active dunes. Coyote brush scrub occurs on the upland areas inland from the active dune system, and is the dominant upland plant community of the Refuge.

Central Foredunes:
The central foredune plant community is typical of dunes in the early stages of colonization and stabilization by plants. Protected somewhat from the wind and from storm surges, the foredunes are commonly stable enough to support a community of low-growing herbaceous and woody perennial plant species. On the Refuge, the northern foredune community occurs on recently stabilized sand dunes above the high tide line. Common species of the northern foredune community include yellow and pink sand verbena (*Abronia latifolia* and *A. umbellata*), silky beach pea (*Lathyrus littoralis*), beach primrose (*Camissonia cheiranthifolia*), sea rocket (*Cakile maritima*), beach morning glory (*Calystegia sordanella*), and beach bur (*Franseria chamissonis* ssp. *bipinnatisecta*, *F. chamissonis* ssp. *chamissonis*). In addition, some seaside buckwheat (*Eriogonum latifolium*) and seacliff buckwheat (*E. parvifolium*) plants occur in the northern portion of the Refuge (John Gilchrist & Associates et al. 1997) (see related discussion in the *Smith's Blue Butterfly* section in *Federally Listed Species at the Refuge* below).

Central Dune Scrub:
Central dune scrub forms on stabilized dunes and coastal bluffs and consists of a dense cover of low, perennial, woody subshrubs and herbs. Dominant plant species of this community include yellow bush lupine (*Lupinus arboreus* ssp. *arboreus*), lizard tail (*Eriophyllum staechadifolium*), sea lettuce (*Dudleya farinosa*), beach bur, mock heather (*Ericameria ericoides* ssp. *ericoides*), seaside buckwheat, and seacliff buckwheat. Monterey spineflower (*Chorizanthe pungens* var. *pungens*), which is federally listed, also occurs in the Refuge's central dune scrub. Other special-status plants reported to occur in this community include Monterey paintbrush (*Castilleja latifolia* var. *latifolia*), branching beach aster (*Coreothogyne leucophylla*), and coast wallflower (*Erysimum ammophilum*) (John Gilchrist & Associates et al. 1997). At the Refuge, central dune scrub occurs on the southwestern border of the Refuge. Central dune scrub on the Refuge is the northern tip of a large contiguous patch of this plant community that extends south on the dune system for more than two miles across private land and onto Marina State Beach.

Coyote Brush Scrub/Grassland:
In the vicinity of the Refuge, coyote brush scrub represents a successional community that has developed following the abandonment of agricultural operations. Although the Refuge land was transferred from U.S. Coast

Guard possession in 1974, upland portions of the reserve were leased for cultivation; later, local farmers were contracted to till the soil and plant barley for wintering waterfowl. Both these practices have ceased since the onset of state budget limitations and drought; the portions of the Refuge where these practices were conducted are in early successional stages. (Cull 1991.) Coyote brush scrub is widespread in the upland areas inland from the Refuge's dunes. The dominant species in this habitat is coyote brush, which forms pure stands in some places. Interspersed within the scrub habitat are large and small patches of grassland dominated by native and nonnative grasses and herbs. Immediately after agriculture ceased, the grassland was dominated by nonnative ruderal species such as poison hemlock (*Conium maculatum*), bristly ox-tongue (*Picris echioides*), field mustard (*Brassica campestris*) and white sweet clover (*Melilotus alba*).

However, intensive restoration efforts by the Watershed Institute in the late 1990s greatly reduced the abundance of nonnative species, replacing them with native annual and perennial grasses such as wild rye (*Elymus glaucus*), California barley (*Hordeum brachyantherum*), annual hairgrass (*Deschampsia caespitosa*), and California brome (*Bromus carinatus*). The native grassland is now maintained through a combination of intensive hand weeding and weed-whacking of exotic species and regular mechanical mowing three to four times each year. Unless burning or other disturbance occurs, the coyote brush is expected to encroach on grassland patches.

Under natural conditions, fire plays an important role in shaping the plant communities of upland habitats in the Monterey Bay area such as coyote brush scrub and grassland. Repeated fires prevent woody species such as coyote brush from colonizing and eventually dominating grasslands. Historic documents suggest that aboriginal populations deliberately set fires annually in coastal prairie habitats around Monterey Bay; fires may also have been inadvertently caused (e.g., Greenlee and Langenheim 1990). Prior to aboriginal settlement, the average interval between fires caused by lightning strikes was probably 2–15 years.

*Wildlife*

The Refuge provides valuable habitat for a diversity of wildlife species, in part because of its location adjacent to other highly productive wetland and marine habitats. Approximately 279 vertebrate species are known or expected to occur in and around the Refuge, including 116 species of waterbirds. More than 50 special-status wildlife species are known or believed to use habitats on the Refuge. Table C-2 (Appendix C) lists all species federally listed as threatened or endangered as well as Birds of Conservation Concern that are known or believed to occur on the Refuge. Birds of Conservation Concern are species identified by the Service that are in need of conservation action to prevent future listings. Under Executive Order 13186, these species represent conservation priorities for the Service and are to be specifically considered during planning.

Wetland Wildlife. The quality of amphibian and reptile habitat offered by the Refuge's wetlands is highly variable. The Salinas River Lagoon is generally too saline to support many amphibians and reptiles. In upstream areas of the Refuge, which have a stronger freshwater influence and more riparian vegetation cover, the following species are reported to occur:

Pacific coast aquatic garter snake (*Thamnophis atratus*), common garter snake (*Thamnophis sirtalis*), western terrestrial garter snake (*Thamnophis elegans*), western fence lizard (*Sceloporus occidentalis*), southern alligator lizard (*Elgaria multicarinata*), sharp-tailed snake (*Contia tenuis*), ringneck snake (*Diadophus punctatus*), common king snake (*Lampropeltis getulus*), California slender salamander (*Batrachoseps attenuatus*), Pacific treefrog (*Pseudacris regilla*), bullfrog (*Rana catesbeiana*), and western toad (*Bufo boreas*).

The Refuge's wetlands provide habitat for numerous resident and migratory bird species. The sandbar at the mouth of the Salinas River Lagoon, the lagoon shoreline, and islands in the lagoon provide important roosting sites for California brown pelican (*Pelecanus occidentalis californicus*) and roosting and nesting sites for western snowy plover (*Charadrius alexandrinus nivosus*), both of which are federally listed. Black skimmer (*Rynchops niger*), a Bird of Conservation Concern,

**California brown pelican (*Pelecanus occidentalis californicus*)**
*Dr. Antonio J. Ferreira Photo*

attempted nesting here in 2000; this site might attract additional pairs of the species in the future.

The wetlands also support stilts, avocets, herons, kingfishers, egrets, terns, gulls, ducks and several other species of waterfowl and shorebirds. During periods of low water, such as late summer, exposed mud and sand provide important foraging habitat for shorebirds. Larger shorebirds, dabbling ducks, herons, and egrets forage in shallow nearshore waters of the lagoon. Areas of deeper water provide foraging for grebes, cormorants, diving ducks, terns and osprey. Areas of northern coastal salt marsh on the Refuge are frequented by a range of species similar to that found in the lagoon, especially those favoring shallow and more saline water. Wintering waterfowl populations on the Refuge vary from 500 to 3,000 depending on the availability of water. Use is also heavy during the spring migration, when as many as 500 dabbling ducks roost and forage in the area. Waterfowl use both the Salinas River and the saline pond. The central coast arroyo willow riparian forest and scrub communities are frequented by insectivorous birds; the larger trees are used as perches by raptors such as northern harrier (*Circus cyaneus*), white-tailed kite (*Elanus caeruleus*), osprey (*Pandion haliaetus*), and barn owl (*Tyto alba*) (John Gilchrist & Associates et al. 1997).

A variety of mammals use the Refuge's wetland habitats. They include: muskrat (*Ondatra zibethica*), beaver (*Castor canadensis*), gray fox (*Urocyon cinereoargenteus*), red fox (*Vulpes vulpes*), striped skunk (*Mephitis mephitis*), longtail weasel (*Mustela frenata*), Virginia opossum (*Didelphis virginiana*), vagrant shrew (*Sorex vagrans*), broad-footed mole (*Scapanus latimanus*), brush rabbit (*Sylvilagus bachmani*), raccoon (*Procyon lotor*), dusky-footed woodrat (*Neotoma fuscipes*), deer mouse (*Peromyscus maniculatus*), and coyote (*Canis latrans*). Foxes and coyotes contribute substantially to predation on ground-nesting birds.

A number of special-status wildlife species may occur in the wetland habitats of the Refuge (see Table C-2 in Appendix C). The Refuge's federally listed species include western snowy plover and California brown pelican; they are discussed further in the *Federally Listed Species* section below. Other special-status species that occur on the Refuge include California brackish water snail (*Tryonia imitator*), Southwestern pond turtle (*Clemmys marmorata pallida*), steelhead (*Oncorhynchus mykiss*), American white pelican (*Pelecanus erythrorhynchos*), double-crested cormorant (*Phalacrocorax auritus*), bufflehead (*Bucephala albeola*), osprey, white-tailed kite, northern harrier, sharp-shinned hawk (*Accipiter striatus*), Cooper's hawk (*Accipiter cooperii*), merlin (*Falco columbarius*), American peregrine falcon (*Falco peregrinus anatum*), whimbrel (*Numenius phaeopus*), long-billed curlew (*Numenius americanus*), marbled godwit (*Limosa fedoa*), short-billed dowitcher (*Limnodromus griseus*), California gull (*Larus californicus*), elegant tern (*Sterna elegans*), black skimmer, short-eared owl (*Asio flammeus*), willow flycatcher (*Empidonax traillii*), California yellow warbler (*Dendroica petechia brewsteri*)), salt marsh wandering shrew (*Sorex vagrans halicoetes*), Monterey ornate shrew (*Sorex ornatus salarius*), and Salinas harvest mouse (*Reithrodontomys megalotis distichlis*).

**California gull**
**(*Larus californicus*)**
*USFWS Photo*

Upland Wildlife. The coyote brush scrub habitat of the Refuge's uplands is used by reptiles, birds, and mammals. Common reptiles that occur in coyote brush scrub and the grassland patches that intergrade with it include the western skink (*Eumeces skiltonianus*), racer (*Coluber constrictor*), gopher snake (*Pituophis melanoleucas*), common king snake, and western terrestrial garter snake. Many birds forage in this habitat, including raptors such as northern harrier, red-tailed hawk (*Buteo jamaicensis*), turkey vulture (*Cathartes aura*), white-tailed kite, osprey, and barn owl. Typical upland mammals include gray and red foxes, longtail weasel, California ground squirrel (*Spermophylis beecheyi*), black-tailed jackrabbit, Botta's pocket gopher (*Thomomys bottae*), deer mouse, and western harvest mouse (*Reithrodontomys megalotis*) (John Gilchrist & Associates et al. 1997).

No federally listed species are known to make significant use of the coyote brush scrub on the Refuge. However, several other special-status wildlife species are reported to use this community, including white-tailed kite, northern harrier, Cooper's hawk, merlin, short-eared owl, Monterey ornate shrew, and Salinas harvest mouse (Appendix C). Grassland restoration efforts on the former cropland site and elsewhere on the Refuge might provide nesting habitat for grasshopper sparrow (a Bird of Conservation Concern) and western meadowlark (a focal species in the Grassland Bird Conservation Plan).

Wildlife of Dunes and Beaches. Because dune and beach habitats are unstable and typically lack fresh water, cover, and forage, they generally support a limited range of wildlife. Birds are the most commonly observed wildlife in these communities. Several bird species use the beaches and dunes of the Refuge for foraging, roosting, and nesting; they include shorebirds, passerines, gulls, and raptors. Other wildlife species observed or expected in the dune and beach habitats of the Refuge are western fence lizard, gopher snake, deer mouse, gray fox, red fox, and longtail weasel.

Three federally listed species are reported to occur in the dune and beach areas of the Refuge: Smith's blue butterfly, western snowy plover, and California brown pelican (Appendix C). They are discussed further in *Federally Listed Species* below. In addition, the northern foredune and central dune scrub communities provide suitable habitat for other special-status species, including the globose dune beetle (*Coelus globosus*), black legless lizard (*Anniella pulchra nigra*), American white pelican, merlin, peregrine falcon, long-billed curlew, whimbrel, marbled godwit, short-billed dowitcher, California gull, and elegant tern.

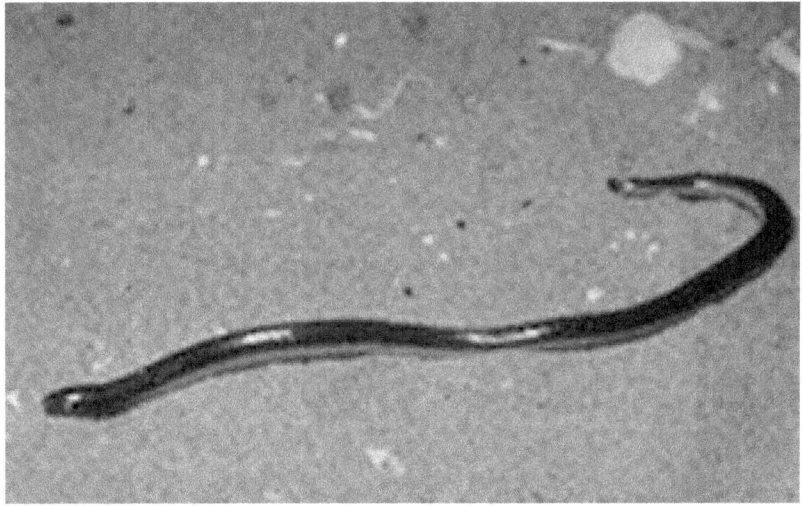

**Black legless lizard (*Anniella pulchra nigra*)**
*John H. Tashjian Photo*

Wildlife in the Salinas River Lagoon. The composition of the fish population in the Salinas River Lagoon is typical of that found in lagoon/rivermouth habitats elsewhere on the central California coast. Native freshwater fish found in the occasionally brackish water of the lagoon include: Sacramento blackfish (*Orthodon microlepidotus*), Sacramento sucker (*Catostomus occidentalis*), Sacramento squawfish (*Ptychocheilus grandis*), California roach (*Lavinia exilicauda*), threespine stickleback (*Gasterosteus aculeatus*) and steelhead/rainbow trout (*Oncorhynchus mykiss*). These species have varying tolerances for saline water; migrating steelhead may use the lagoon to acclimatize themselves to changes in salinity between ocean and river.

Introduced freshwater species that can occur in the Salinas River Lagoon include: carp (*Cyprinus carpo*), white bass (*Morone chrysops*), bluegill (*Lepomis macrochirus*), green sunfish (*Lepomis cyanellus*), mosquitofish (*Gambusia affinis*) and threadfin shad (*Dorosoma petenense*).

Saltwater fish are also found in the Salinas River Lagoon. Some saltwater species are found year-round; others are typical of periods when the sandbar at the mouth of the lagoon is breached, creating an open connection with Pacific waters. Year-round users of the lagoon include small numbers of starry flounders (*Platichthyes stellatus*) and staghorn sculpin (*Leptocottus armatus*). Adults of these species spawn in the ocean but juveniles often use the lagoon to rear for as much as a year. During periods of saltwater connectivity, saltwater species commonly found in the lagoon include: Pacific herring (*Clupea harengus*), topsmelt (*Atherinops affinis*), shiner surfperch (*Cymatogaster aggregata*), walleye surfperch (*Hyperprosopon argenteum*), silver surfperch (*H. ellipticum*), spotfin surfperch (*H. anale*), white surfperch (*Phanerodon furcatus*), surf smelt (*Hypomesus pretiosus*), northern anchovy (*Engralis mordax*), jacksmelt (*Atherinopsis californiensis*), English sole (*Parophrys vetulus*), and striped bass (*Morone saxatilis*). Green sturgeon (*Acipenser medirostris*) are also thought to occur occasionally.

Invertebrates. Invertebrate surveys have not been conducted for the Refuge. However, based on surveys of nearby sites with habitats similar to those on the Refuge, it is likely that invertebrates are abundant at the Refuge. Tube-dwelling amphipods (*Corophium* spp.), water boatmen (*Corixidae*), and the amphipods of the algal mats and pondweed (*Eogammarus* spp.) are all known to be abundant in the Salinas River Lagoon.

## Federally Listed Species at the Refuge

The following sections provide more information on selected special-status species that are known to occur or that may occur at the Refuge. Because the Refuge is charged with the mission of management for the benefit of federally listed species, this section focuses on federally listed species. Appendix C provides an overview of all special-status species known or expected to occur on the Refuge, including State-listed species and State species of special concern.

Monterey Gilia (*Gilia tenuiflora* ssp. *arenaria*). Monterey gilia is an annual herb in the phlox family (*Polemoniaceae*), and is federally listed as endangered. It is known from about 15 locations in coastal Monterey County, including Marina State Beach, Sunset State Beach, Salinas River State Beach, Fort Ord, the Refuge, and some private properties south of the Refuge (California Department of Fish and Game 2000). The occurrence at the Refuge represents the northernmost documented population of the species. Monterey gilia is thought by some botanists to intergrade with the greater yellowthroat gilia (*Gilia tenuiflora* ssp. *tenuiflora*) where the two subspecies co-occur near the mouth of the Salinas River. Monterey gilia is found on sandy soils in openings within maritime chaparral, cismontane woodland, coastal sand dunes, and coastal scrub communities. Within the Refuge, Monterey gilia is expected to be found in open patches within dune scrub, preferring relatively stable sites that have some leaf litter accumulation and soil development, that offer protection from high winds and salt spray, and `that experience no wave or storm-surge activity. It was documented on the

Refuge in 1992 by the California Native Plant Society (California Native Plant Society 1992); however, more surveys are needed to map its locations and estimate its population size. Threats to the species include small mammal herbivory, loss of habitat because of development and sand mining, and invasion by nonnative plants (U.S. Fish and Wildlife Service 1998).

Menzies' Wallflower (*Erysimum menziesii*). Menzies' wallflower is a perennial or biennial herb of the mustard family (*Brassicaceae*) and is federally listed as endangered. Since the original listing of Menzies' wallflower in 1992, several new subspecies have been recognized. The Service considers the following subspecies as included in the original listing of Menzies' wallflower: *Erysimum menziesii* ssp. *menziesii*, *E. m.* ssp. *yadonii*, and *E. m.* ssp. *eurekense* (U.S. Fish and Wildlife Service 1998). Populations of Menzies' wallflower in the vicinity of the Refuge include those at Marina State Beach and on several private properties near Marina (California Department of Fish and Game 2000). Several populations of the subspecies *E. m.* ssp. *yadonii*, Yadon's wallflower, are known from coastal dunes and coastal strands along Monterey Bay in the vicinity of the Refuge; they bloom between May and September. Threats to the wallflower include natural disturbances such as storm surges, changes in the course of the Salinas River, habitat loss because of development and sand mining, off-road vehicle traffic, trampling, and invasion of nonnative species such as common ice plant (*Carpobrotus edulis*, *C. chilense*).

**Menzies' wallflower (*Erysimum menziesii*)**
*Brother Alfred Brousseau Photo*

Menzies' wallflower is not known to occur on the Refuge but suitable habitat exists. Further surveys are needed to confirm its absence from the Refuge. A historic occurrence of Yadon's wallflower within the Refuge may have been extirpated by storm surges and changes in the Salinas River mouth, as a recent field survey failed to locate any individuals on the Refuge (John Gilchrist & Associates et al. 1997). The beach strand and foredunes on the Refuge offer suitable habitat for both wallflower subspecies, in locations that are above the high-tide line and protected from wave action (U.S. Fish and Wildlife Service 1998).

Monterey Spineflower (*Chorizanthe pungens* var. *pungens*). The Monterey spineflower is an annual herb in the buckwheat family (*Polygonaceae*), and is federally listed as threatened. The spineflower occurs near the coast in northern Monterey County and southern Santa Cruz County. It is found in a wide range of habitats but prefers openings on sandy soils in maritime chaparral, oak woodland, coastal dunes, coastal scrub, and grassland communities (California Department of Fish and Game 2000). In grasslands, the species occurs along road margins, in fuel breaks, and on other disturbed sites (U.S. Army Corps of Engineers 1992). The normal blooming period for the spineflower is mid- to late spring (April–June). Threats to the Monterey spineflower include loss of habitat as a result of development, and invasion by nonnative plants, especially common ice plant (U.S. Fish and Wildlife Service 1998).

Monterey spineflower was observed on the Refuge in 1992 and again in 2001 (California Native Plant Society 1992, 2001). Systematic surveys for the species on the Refuge are still needed because the extent of this population is unknown. The Refuge supports suitable habitat for the Monterey spineflower on open, sandy patches on active dunes and in dune scrub communities. Several populations are also known from the vicinity of the Refuge. Most of the known extant populations are found on the undeveloped western portions of the U.S. Army's Fort Ord (U.S. Army Corps of Engineers 1992). Other known occurrences near the Refuge include those at Marina State Beach, Sunset State Beach, Manresa State Beach, Asilomar State Beach, Fort Ord Dunes State Park, Manzanita County Park, and various locations along U.S. 101 (California Department of Fish and Game 2000).

**Monterey spineflower (*Chorizanthe pungens*)**
*Brother Alfred Brousseau Photo*

Smith's Blue Butterfly (*Euphilotes enoptes smithi*). Smith's blue butterfly is federally listed as endangered. It is found in coastal dune scrub and coastal sage scrub plant communities at several Monterey County localities; the Refuge represents the northern limit of the species' range. Both the larval and adult stages of Smith's blue butterfly rely on seaside buckwheat (*Eriogonum latifolium*) and seacliff buckwheat (*E. parvifolium*) host plants for food. After hatching, the larvae feed for several weeks and then molt to a pupal stage that lasts ten months. Adults emerge in late summer and early autumn to mate and lay eggs on buckwheat flowers. At the Refuge, seaside buckwheat and seacliff buckwheat occur in the central dune scrub and northern foredune vegetation communities, and the Refuge supports a population of Smith's blue butterfly of unknown size. Threats to the species in the vicinity of the Refuge include habitat loss because of land development, and damage to remaining habitat as a result of offroad vehicle use and invasion by nonnative plants such as common ice plant and European beach grass (*Ammophila arenaria*). The Service has identified securing the coastal sand dunes at the Refuge as essential to the recovery of the Smith's blue butterfly (U.S. Fish and Wildlife Service 1984).

Steelhead (*Oncorhynchus mykiss*). The steelhead is federally listed as threatened. Steelhead may be present in small numbers in the Salinas River and the Salinas River Lagoon; they were collected in the Salinas River Lagoon during intensive sampling in 1963 and again in 1991 (John Gilchrist & Associates et al. 1997). Additional surveys for steelhead should be carried out on the Refuge. Steelhead in the Salinas River are part of the South-Central California Coast Evolutionarily Significant Unit (ESU) listed by the National Marine Fisheries Service (NMFS), which has designated the Salinas River Basin as critical habitat for this ESU of steelhead.

Suitable habitat for steelhead is greatly limited in the Salinas River system, in part because yearly flows in the lower reaches of the river are extremely variable and water temperatures are inhospitably high during low-flow periods, and also because the migration required to reach upstream spawning and rearing habitats is excessively long. Steelhead are known to use Arroyo Seco and the Nacimiento and San Antonio Rivers when access is possible. However, these tributaries join the Salinas River 40, 80, and 80 miles upstream from its mouth, respectively.

Western Snowy Plover (*Charadrius alexandrinus nivosus*). The western snowy plover is a small, pale-colored shorebird that ranges from southern Washington to Baja California del Sur, Mexico. It is also known from inland lakes in the western U.S., although the birds that breed at interior lakes are considered mostly disjunct from the coastal population (U.S. Fish and Wildlife Service 1993b). The Pacific coast population of the western snowy plover is federally listed as threatened.

The plover inhabits open beaches in marine, estuarine, and lacustrine settings. It nests in sandy or gravelly substrates such as sand dunes and forages for invertebrates on wet, sandy shorelines and receding lake or estuary margins. Its breeding season extends from mid-March though mid-September.

The Refuge is home to an important breeding population of western snowy plovers. This population consists of a combination of year-round residents and migratory birds that are present only during the breeding season. Migratory plovers may winter in southern California or in coastal Mexico. The birds typically return to the same nest locations each year, although individual nests are generally not reused because of the unstable and shifting nature of coastal dunes. At the Refuge, foraging and nesting areas include the beach strand and foredunes, the unvegetated margins of northern coastal salt marsh habitat, saline pond, and sandy islands within the Salinas River and Salinas River Lagoon.

The primary predators of snowy plover adults, chicks, and eggs at the Refuge include nonnative red foxes, free-roaming cats, skunks, northern harriers, kestrels, and gulls. Other potential threats to nesting success include high winds, storm surges, domestic dogs, and crushing by vehicles or pedestrians (John Gilchrist & Associates et al. 1997).

In 1984, Point Reyes Bird Observatory began monitoring and collecting data on breeding plovers on the Refuge. Data from successive years revealed a drastic decline in plover nest success. Nesting attempts decreased from 40 in 1986 to 24 in 1990. In addition, from 1988 to 1990, mammalian predation accounted for a loss of 47% of all nests found on the Refuge (Point Reyes Bird Observatory file data).

During the 1991 breeding season, Refuge personnel began protecting individual plover nests with fencing (exclosures) in an attempt to decrease predation and human impacts. As a result, nest success increased from 10% in 1987 to approximately 83% in 1994. However, as the use of exclosures continued through the 1992 and 1993 breeding seasons, it became apparent that while exclosures increased nest success they also caused increased adult mortality and possibly decreased chick survival. Between 1991 and 1993, the percentage of chicks fledged per successful hatch (chick fledging rate) decreased below that of the pre-exclosure period; it is believed that predators learned to recognize and target nest exclosures. In addition, both adult and juvenile plovers were at risk from mammalian predators, in particular the nonnative red fox, when they left the nest exclosure.

In an effort to increase fledging success and reduce adult mortality, the Refuge implemented an integrated predator management program in 1994. The plan combined the use of exclosures in high-risk areas with the removal of problem mammalian predators. Nest success and fledging rates both increased in 1994. In addition, adult mortality decreased from 3 in 1992 and 7 in 1993 to zero in 1994. As a result, the Refuge continued the predator management plan in subsequent breeding years.

Nest success has continued to increase from 45% in 1995 to 70% in 1999. However, after an initial increase, the fledging rate again began to decrease by 1999, primarily because of predation by northern harrier; the 1996–2000 fledge rate was 22%. After reviewing the data, the Refuge implemented a three-year avian predator management experiment in 1999. The goal of this experiment was to increase snowy plover fledge rates by capturing and relocating problem avian predators, including northern harrier, kestrel, and loggerhead shrike individuals. Following the 2000 breeding season, the results were evaluated and used to develop an avian predator management program (see Appendix H). This program will be added to the existing predator management plan.

California Brown Pelican (*Pelecanus occidentalis californicus*). The brown pelican ranges from Central California to Chile; California populations are federally listed as endangered. The brown pelican is the smallest of the pelican species. Nonetheless, it weighs as much as 10 pounds, has a 7½-foot wingspan, and can hold up to 3 gallons of water and fish in its bill pouch. Pelicans forage by flying above shallow, coastal marine waters, finding fish with their keen eyesight, and then diving. They rarely venture far out to sea or far inland. Typically social birds, they nest and roost communally in most years.

The breeding range of the California brown pelican extends from the Channel Islands in southern California south to the state of Nayarit, Mexico. After the breeding season, California brown pelicans disperse along the Pacific coast, ranging as far north as southern British Columbia and as far south as Colima, Mexico. Pelicans are most abundant along the central California coast between July and November (Shuford et al. 1989).

During the nonbreeding season, the central California coast, including the Refuge, becomes important for communal roosting. At the Refuge, California brown pelicans use portions of the beach strand, islands in the Salinas River Lagoon, and the lagoon side of the lagoon-mouth sandspit for day roost areas (John Gilchrist & Associates et al. 1997). Roosting flocks are common at the mouth of the Salinas River and on the islands near the river mouth from April through December. As many as 1,400 pelicans have been observed roosting at the river mouth.

Historic threats to the California brown pelican include loss of nesting habitat, disturbance of nesting and roosting sites, egg harvesting, and the use of DDT, which reduced eggshell strength; pelicans were also killed by fishermen. While these threats have largely been removed and Atlantic coast populations have been delisted by the Service, there are still only about 5,000 breeding pairs of brown pelicans in California, and California populations remain endangered.

California Least Tern (*Sterna antillarum browni*). The California least tern is federally listed as endangered. The species ranges from Baja California northward through the San Francisco Bay area, but nesting is currently restricted to a few sites from San Francisco Bay south to San Diego County. Least terns prefer sparsely vegetated, open, sandy areas. Their nesting habitat is similar to that of the western snowy plover and they are known to nest in close proximity to snowy plovers. Least terns occur on the Refuge as occasional spring migrants and likely forage in the surf adjacent to the Refuge. Although the Refuge provides suitable nesting habitat, there have been no records of nesting terns on the Refuge since 1937 (Roberson and Tenney 1993).

Southern Sea Otter (*Enhydra lutris nereis*). The southern sea otter is federally listed as threatened. The species ranges from Pigeon Point in southern San Mateo County to Purisima Point in Santa Barbara County, but is occasionally observed north and south of its typical range (Zeiner et al. 1990). Southern sea otters generally remain within about 1 mile of the shoreline. They rest and groom in kelp forests, and dive to forage for sea urchins, crabs, clams, mussels, abalone, and other shellfish. Southern sea otters can be observed in the offshore areas in the vicinity of the Refuge (outside the Refuge's mean high water boundary), but they are more likely to be seen in areas where kelp beds are more abundant, such as the northern and

**Sea otter (*Enhydra lutris*)**
*Dr. Lloyd Glenn Ingles Photo*

southern portions of Monterey Bay, which have a rocky substrate. Historically, the southern sea otter was threatened by overhunting for its fur, and the population was reduced to about 50 animals along the Big Sur coast in the early twentieth century. There are approximately 2000 sea otters in California today. The population appears to be recovering, but the sea otter is still at risk from oil spills, collisions with power boats, drowning in fishing nets, and disease.

## Cultural Resources

### Cultural Setting

Prehistoric Context. Based on certain characteristic artifacts, archaeologists working in the Monterey Bay region commonly divide the area's prehistoric record into five time periods (Breschini and Haversat 1980 in Moratto 1984, Jones and Hylkema 1988, Dietz et al. 1988, Milliken et al. 1999). These are:

- The Millingstone Period (8,500–5000 years ago),
- The Early Period (~5,000–2,600 years ago),
- The Middle Period (~2,600–1,250 years ago),
- The Middle/Late Transition (1,250–850 years ago), and
- The Late Period (<850 years ago).

The Millingstone Period (8,500–5000 years ago) is named for the flat stones widely used as grinding surfaces, with a fist-sized handstone as the grinding implement; millingstones are a characteristic artifact in deposits of this age. The Millingstone Period is best represented on the southern California coast, where sites of this age typically contain dense shell middens and large numbers of millingstones and handstones. The Millingstone Period appears to be sparsely represented in the Monterey Bay area, and Milliken et al. (1999) hypothesize that the Refuge area may have been inundated by the sea level rise resulting from melting of Wisconsinan glacial ice at the end of the Pleistocene Epoch (~10,000 years ago). However, Jones and Jones (1992) have identified a component dating to this period at a site near Moss Landing.

Deposits of the Early Period (~5,000–2,600 years ago) are characterized by the presence of large square-stemmed and side-notched projectile points, mortars and pestles, and millingstones and handstones. During the Early Period, the Monterey Bay area was inhabited by people whose archeological signature has been identified as the Sur Pattern (Breschini and Haversat 1980, Moratto 1984, Milliken et al. 1999).

The Middle Period (~2,600–1,250 years ago) is the most commonly represented period in the Monterey Bay region. It is typically associated with smaller projectile points, mortars and pestles, saucer-shaped shell beads, and a variety of bone artifacts. This archeological signature has been identified as the Monterey Pattern (Breschini and Haversat 1984, Moratto 1984, Milliken et al. 1999).

The period from about 1,250 to 850 years ago is referred to as the Middle/Late Transition. During this time, the Monterey Bay area appears to have been used as a coastal collector destination. Sedentary village sites were located in the interior.

The Late Period (<850 years ago) is poorly represented in the Monterey Bay region. It appears to be typified by small side-notched and serrated projectile points, mortars and pestles, and split-punched shell beads. After 400 years ago, clam shell disk beads are also represented. Following

European contact, glass trade beads appear in the record (Milliken et al. 1999).

<u>Ethnographic Context</u>. The peoples who inhabited northern Monterey County prior to the European influx have been called the Costanoans. The term Costanoan is derived from the Spanish Costaños, meaning Coast People (Kroeber 1925). The Costanoans are a linguistically defined group composed of several autonomous groups speaking eight different but related languages; anthropologists have referred to these groups as *tribelets* (Levy 1978). The area that is now the Refuge may have been inhabited by the Calendarruc tribelet (Milliken 1988).

Many Native American descendants of the original peoples of the Monterey Bay area refer to themselves as Ohlone; the term Ohlonean has been used as a synonym for Costanoan (Milliken 1988). The origin of the root *Ohlone* is uncertain. Margolin (1978) has suggested that it is derived from a Miwok word meaning *western people*, or from the name of a village along the San Mateo coast.

The territory of the Costanoan or Ohlone people extended along the coast from San Francisco Bay in the north to a point immediately south of Carmel, and stretched about 60 miles inland. This area encompasses a significant length of coastline as well as several inland valleys (Breschini et al. 1983). The Costanoans were gatherer-hunters, relying heavily on a wide range of foods, including acorns, sea foods, seeds, berries, roots, land and sea mammals, waterfowl, reptiles, and insects (Levy 1978).

<u>Historic Setting</u>.
Spanish Period:
In 1542, Spanish explorer Juan Rodríguez Cabrillo sailed up the California coast in search of the Northwest Passage. Although Cabrillo may have sighted the headland of Monterey Bay, the first European known to have seen the bay was Sebastián Rodríguez Cermeño, who sailed along its shores while searching for an appropriate location for the establishment of a northern Spanish port on the California coast in 1595. In 1602, Sebastian Vizcaíno became the second European to enter Monterey Bay and the first to make a landing there. Vizcaíno's enthusiastic descriptions of the bay gave impetus for the overland expeditions of Gaspar de Portolá (1769–70), who along with Fathers Crespí and Serra founded Mission San Carlos Borroméo, which was moved to its present Carmel site in 1771, and the Presidio of Monterey (Fink 1978, Hart 1978, Hoover 1990).

Eager to establish pueblo settlements and consolidate its political claim to Alta California, the Spanish government authorized the distribution of lands surrounding the mission and presidio to Spanish settlers who would devote themselves to farming and stock raising. By 1793, several pueblo lots and land grants of as much as three leagues (approximately 13,200 acres) had been authorized around Mission San Carlos Borroméo and along the Salinas River. They were awarded both to civilians and to retired soldiers. Some of these lots may have included lands now within the Refuge. The principal economic activities in the region included cattle ranching, agriculture, and various mission-based industries, such as weaving, blacksmithing, masonry, carpentry, hide curing, and tallow rendering. The bulk of the labor was provided by local Native Americans. Agriculture was confined mainly to the mission lands where irrigation systems had been constructed (Fink 1978, Hoover et al. 1990, Swernoff 1981).

Mexican Period:
The fertile lands in the vicinity of the Salinas River mouth attracted a succession of Mexican ranchers and farmers. Located near the mouth of the Salinas River near the present town of Castroville, Rancho Rincón de las Salinas extended from just east of Twin Bridges to the Pacific Ocean. This 2,220-acre tract, which contained the current Refuge, was granted to Cristina Delgado by Governor Figueroa in 1833. Rafael Estrada acquired the property in 1853 (Beck and Haase 1974, Hoover et al. 1990).

United States Acquisition and Settlement:
The American acquisition of California brought many changes to the Monterey Bay area. The port town of Monterey had been visited by American and other foreign traders during the Spanish and Mexican periods, and had been home to the only United States consul to Alta California, Thomas Larkin. Since Monterey had served as the territorial capital during both Spanish and Mexican periods, the town was pivotal in the transition to American governance. In 1849, the Constitutional Convention met at Colton Hall in Monterey to establish the State government. Over the ensuing decades, a thriving commercial fishing and whaling industry emerged in the coastal regions of Monterey County (established 1850) alongside the growing agricultural economy of the Salinas River valley.

United States Military at the Refuge:
Lands that now make up the Refuge have a significant history of use by the United States military. The U.S. Navy acquired the property in 1942, and established coastal defense fortifications there during World War II. In 1952, the Navy transferred the property to the U.S. Coast Guard. In 1967, approximately 270 acres of the Refuge (all land north of the current trail system) was again transferred, this time to the U.S. Army, who used the site to create the Castroville Amphibious Training Area. The southern portion of the Refuge (approximately 94 acres) remained under U.S. Coast Guard jurisdiction as their Castroville Radio Direction Finder Station. The Coast Guard site was actively farmed in artichokes until operations ceased in 1973. The entire property was then transferred to the Department of the Interior on July 10, 1973. It was managed by the California Department of Fish and Game as a wildlife management area until 1991, when the U.S. Fish and Wildlife Service began managing the site as part of the National Wildlife Refuge System. All surface structures except a WWII bomb shelter were removed from the site prior to transfer to the Department of the Interior.

The 54th Coast Artillery Regiment, an African-American unit, was transferred to the west coast in 1942 (Breschini et al. 1996). A battery of the 54th Regiment was stationed in the Moss Landing area. Remains of the unit's camp have been recorded approximately 4 miles north of the Refuge (Breschini et al. 1996). It is unknown whether this unit operated on the Refuge or whether evidence of their use of the site is found on the Refuge.

Cultural Resource Sites on the Refuge. Very little formal cultural resources survey work has been conducted on the Refuge. One structure on the Refuge may be eligible for listing on the National Register of Historic Places (National Register): the World War II–era bomb shelter located near the parking lot. Another feature of possible interest is a barge marked *Sauce Bros* that grounded offshore of the northwest corner of the Refuge after a storm in December 1983. Neither the barge nor the bomb shelter has been formally evaluated or recorded; additional evaluation is necessary. In addition, because there has been no survey of historic resources on the Refuge, it is unknown whether other sites on the Refuge are eligible for listing in the National Register.

Archaeological Sites in the Vicinity. Several archaeological sites have been recorded and excavated in the general vicinity of the Refuge. Perhaps the two most thoroughly documented are prehistoric archaeological sites (Dondero 1984, Dietz et al. 1988, Jones and Jones 1992, Milliken et al. 1999). Information from these sites has added to a regional understanding of burial practices, subsistence practices, and inter-regional trade (Milliken et al. 1999). Of note is that archaeological evidence from one of these sites indicates that fur seals were probably hunted in rookeries; this is significant because fur seal rookeries are historically known to occur only in more northern latitudes (Milliken et al. 1999).

## Social Environment

### Land Use

Overview. The Refuge is surrounded almost entirely by rural and open-space land uses, but the Refuge is near several important population centers, including the City of Castroville (about 2.5 miles to the east) and the City of Monterey (about 11 miles to the south) (Figure 1). Land uses adjacent to the Refuge include Salinas River State Beach to the north; private lands, including agricultural fields (artichokes) and coastal sand dunes, to the east and south; and, to the west, the open ocean of Monterey Bay.

Agricultural Activities. Agriculture has historically been the mainstay of Monterey County's economy, and it remains one of the County's largest economic sectors. The total market value of agricultural production in Monterey County was almost $2.3 billion in 1998 (Monterey County Agricultural Commissioner's Office 1999). Major crops grown in the County include artichokes, grapes, lettuce, strawberries, and a variety of nursery crops (Monterey County Agricultural Commissioner's Office 1999).

### Traffic and Public Access

The entrance to the Refuge is located approximately 0.5 mile west of Del Monte Boulevard, which exits off of State Highway 1. Access to the Refuge is provided by a private, unimproved agricultural road. An easement allows visitors to access the Refuge via the roadway, but road conditions can be challenging, and during the winter rainy season the road is typically usable only by 4-wheel-drive vehicles. Agricultural equipment and farmworkers' vehicles use the roadway all year; however, agricultural use is heaviest during the peak growing and harvesting season (October–May) (Barr pers. comm.). The Refuge can also be accessed from the north or south along the beach.

**Entrance signs at Salinas River NWR**
*Jones & Stokes Photo*

The quality of service provided by a roadway is described by its level of service (LOS), using a letter rating system to describe peak-period driving conditions. The letters A through F represent progressively worse driving conditions. Generally, LOS A indicates free-flow operation with little or no delay, and LOS F denotes jammed flow with substantial delay.

Traffic volumes along State Highway 1 near the Refuge average approximately 43,000 vehicles per day and the roadway operates at LOS B (California Department of Transportation 1999). Traffic counts along the portion of Del Monte Boulevard near the Refuge are not available. However, it is estimated that this segment of Del Monte Boulevard currently operates at a similar level of service.

*Recreation*
Recreational Activities at the Refuge. Waterfowl hunting, access to fishing, and nonconsumptive uses such as wildlife viewing and photography are the primary activities currently occurring at the Refuge. While some nonmotorized boating (canoeing and kayaking) currently takes place along the Salinas River, the Refuge has no developed boat launching facilities and most boating originates from upstream areas (Barr pers. comm.).

The Refuge provides access to the beach where surf fishing and hiking occur. Fishing in the Salinas River is prohibited. Wildlife viewing and photography is allowed on the Refuge only from designated trails (Figure 2). Dogs and horses are prohibited from the Refuge. Most of the Refuge is closed to public use in an effort to protect rare and endangered species.

The Refuge is one of two sites in the local area open for seasonal public waterfowl hunting typically from October through January, and is the only local site offering walk-in hunting opportunities. The Refuge encompasses approximately 120 acres along the Salinas River that would be conducive to hunting; hunting is currently permitted in an area of approximately 45 acres (3,600 linear feet of riverbank; Figure 2).

Species hunted include geese, ducks, coots, and common moorhen. The Refuge is a key resource for local waterfowl hunters. The nearest alternative location for public waterfowl hunting is the Moss Landing Wildlife Area, approximately 10 miles to the north, which can only be accessed by boat, and other public hunting areas such as the San Luis National Wildlife Refuge near the community of Los Banos are located 80 miles or more away.

Facilities at the Refuge. Because no overnight parking or camping is allowed at the Refuge, existing facilities are limited to an isolated, unpaved parking area and several walking trails (Figure 2). The parking area is small and can only accommodate an estimated 14–18 vehicles during the summer months. During the winter months, when the parking area is wet, capacity falls to an estimated 5–6 parking spaces (Barr pers. comm.). The Refuge has no restroom or picnic facilities and recreationists must carry their own trash off the Refuge. Interpretive signs at the Refuge are limited to one informational sign listing allowed uses, which is located at the entrance to the Refuge. The Refuge has no telephone available for public use.

**Waterfowl hunting on a national wildlife refuge**
*USFWS Photo*

There are several safety concerns related to existing facilities at the Refuge. The Refuge entrance is gated to prevent unauthorized vehicle entry, but the gate does not prevent pedestrian trespassers from entering illegally after the Refuge is closed for the day (Barr pers. comm.). Cars parked in the isolated parking lot are occasionally vandalized or burglarized. In addition, an abandoned concrete bomb shelter is used as a camping area by the homeless and also serves as an illegal firearms target practice area (Barr pers. comm.).

Recreational Use. Table 5 shows an estimated breakdown of recreational use at the Refuge by activity, based on observations by Refuge staff (no formal use surveys have been conducted on the Refuge to date). Based on these estimates of use, recreational use at the Refuge averages between 4,010 and 6,380 visitors per year, which is considered low by comparison with use at other nearby parks and recreation sites. Weekday use at the Refuge in particular is low; weekend use is higher. Overall use at the Refuge peaks at the start of the winter hunting season. Permits for hunting access are not issued for the Refuge. However, hunting use is effectively limited to an estimated 15 hunters per day, as hunting is only permitted on a small portion of the Refuge (Figure 2) (Barr pers. comm.). The Service estimates that approximately 250 hunter-visits take place annually. Visits are estimated to last an average of six hours each, for a total of 1,500 hunting activity hours annually. In the 1995–1996 and 1997–1998 hunting seasons, as many as 8–10 hunters were present on the Refuge at any one time. Hunting use is greatest on the weekends and on Wednesdays.

**Table 5. Estimates of annual recreation use at the Salinas River National Wildlife Refuge.**

| Activity | Peak Use Period | Estimates of Use (visitors per day) |
|---|---|---|
| waterfowl hunting | October  January | 4 6* |
| surf fishing | year round | 6 10 |
| nonconsumptive use | year round (heavier during waterfowl migration periods) | 4 6 |

* Up to approximately 15 hunters/day use the Refuge at the beginning of the hunt season.

Source: Barr (pers. comm.)

As shown in Table 6, visitation at the Refuge is fairly low compared to that at other local recreation areas. This may reflect the different management priorities in operation on State parklands and Refuge lands.  The mission of the State Parks is recreation-oriented, so nearby State parks offer a wider range of nonconsumptive uses (e.g., equestrian uses, windsurfing, hang-gliding, and camping) than the Refuge. In addition, in keeping with their recreational mission, nearby State Beaches are more easily accessed than the Refuge, particularly during the winter rainy season, and offer more public use facilities such as restrooms and picnic tables. Recreation opportunities on the Refuge reflect the wildlife-oriented mission of the Service and the National Wildlife Refuge System.  As a result, while the range of uses available on the Refuge is narrower than in nearby State parks, the Refuge provides opportunities for various types of recreation, including waterfowl hunting, that are not available at other nearby sites.

**Table 6. Recreation use at public parks along the coast near the Refuge.**

| Facility | Size (acres) | Estimated Annual Visitor Use | Consumptive Activities | Non-Consumptive Activities |
|---|---|---|---|---|
| Salinas River NWR | 367 | 4,370 6,900 | Access to fishing, waterfowl hunting | Wildlife viewing and photography |
| Marina State Beach | 131 | 843,100 | None | Hang gliding, kiting, picnicking |
| Moss Landing State Beach | 55 | 73,030 | Fishing | Wildlife viewing, equestrian uses, surfing, windsurfing, picnicking, camping |
| Salinas River State Beach | 246 | 71,635 | Fishing | Wildlife viewing |
| Zmudowski State Beach | 177 | 35,635 | Fishing | wildlife viewing and equestrian uses |

Source: California State Parks, Monterey, California (2000).

# Chapter 5. Plan Implementation

Once the preferred management alternative has been finalized, the CCP has been approved, and the Service has notified the public of its decision, the implementation phase of the CCP process will begin. During the next 15 years, the objectives and strategies presented in this CCP will be realized; the CCP will serve as the primary reference document for all Refuge planning, operations, and management until it is formally revised at the end of this period. The Service will implement the final CCP with assistance from existing and new partner agencies and organizations and from the public.

Activities needed to realize the management strategies discussed in this CCP are referred to as projects. Every effort will be made to implement these projects by the deadlines established here. However, the timing of implementation of the management activities proposed in this document is contingent upon a variety of factors, including:
- Funding,
- Staffing,
- Compliance with other Federal regulations,
- Partnerships, and
- The results of monitoring and evaluation.

Each of these factors is described briefly below as it applies to the Service's proposed action.

## Funding and Personnel

To implement the proposed action and to achieve the objectives and goals of this CCP, the Service will need additional funding and staff. Table 11 describes the budget proposals and staffing needs for the Refuge for each project proposed in this CCP. Projects include: upgrades of existing facilities (e.g., covering the parking lot with a gravel surface), construction of new facilities or amenities (orientation kiosk and interpretive signs), species and habitat monitoring, and management actions such as grassland mowing, prescribed burning, and avian predator translocation. Full implementation of all of the projects proposed in this CCP would require that the Refuge increase its current annual budget by 156% to approximately $320,000.

If the proposed action is implemented, full staffing for both the Salinas River NWR and the nearby Ellicott Slough NWR would include the following.
- Full-time Refuge Manager
- Full-time Refuge Biologist
- Full-time Biological Science Technician
- Full-time Park Ranger
- Part-time Maintenance Worker

In addition, an intern may be hired to help conduct habitat and species inventories and monitoring and to coordinate the new docent program.

**Table 7. Budget proposal for Salinas River NWR Comprehensive Conservation Plan.**

| Project Title | Priority[1] | Start Year | Completion Year | Duration (years) | Operational Cost for Startup (thousands) | Average Annual Cost (thousands) | 15 Year Total Cost (thousands) | Staffing (FTE/ Grade[2]) | RONS[3] |
|---|---|---|---|---|---|---|---|---|---|
| Control nonnative plants on foredunes. | H | 2002 | 2017 | 15 | 5.0 | 14.5 | 222.5 | 0.1/GS 9 0.1/GS 11 | 97704 |
| Develop partnerships with neighboring landowners to control nonnative vegetation on their coastal dunes. | M | 2002 | 2017 | 15 | | 3.2 | 48.0 | 0.05/GS 11 | n/a |
| Install "Closed Area" signs at the boundary of sensitive dune habitat. | H | 2002 | 2017 | 15 | 8.0 | 3.6 | 62.0 | 0.05/GS 7 | 00701 97702 |
| Develop and implement a docent program. | H | 2002 | 2017 | 15 | 45.0 | 17.0 | 300.0 | 0.3/GS 7 0.05/GS 9 | 00701 |
| Install symbolic fencing through the foredune habitat. | H | 2005 | 2017 | 12 | 15.0 | 6.0 | 81.0 | 0.05/GS 5 0.05/GS 7 | 97703 |
| Increase the presence of enforcement officers during plover breeding season. | M | 2002 | 2017 | 15 | | 8.5 | 127.5 | 0.2/GS 7 | 00701 |
| Continue to implement the Monterey Integrated Predator Management Program on the Refuge. | H | 2002 | 2017 | 15 | | 40.0 | 600.0 | 0.1/GS 11 | 97701 |
| Implement the Refuge's Avian Predator Management Plan to include relocation of selected birds that prey heavily on plover chicks. | H | 2002 | 2017 | 15 | 7.0 | 22.0 | 337.0 | 0.1/GS 11 | 97701 |
| Complete a 2 year inventory of the special status species that occur on the Refuge. | M | 2003 | 2005 | 2 | 20.0 | 30.0 | 80.0 | 0.2/GS 5 0.1/GS 11 0.3/GS 9 | 97705 |
| Evaluate and prioritize the special status species that occur on the Refuge. | H | 2008 | 2008 | 1 | 5.2 | | 5.2 | 0.1/GS 9 | 97705 |
| Encourage research on each priority special status species on the Refuge. | M | 2002 | 2017 | 15 | | 3.2 | 48.0 | 0.05/GS 11 | 97705 |
| Explore expansion of the current Refuge boundary. | M | 2002 | 2017 | 15 | | 3.2 | 48.0 | 0.05/GS 11 | n/a |
| Continue to plant and maintain riparian trees and shrubs and support restoration partners. | H | 2002 | 2017 | 15 | | 15.0 | 225.0 | 0.1/GS 5 | n/a |
| Develop and implement a long term monitoring strategy to evaluate the survival and density of riparian revegetation. | M | 2002 | 2017 | 15 | 6.2 | 5.5 | 88.7 | 0.1/GS 5 0.05/GS 9 | 97705 |
| Continue to mow the grassland annually and apply herbicide to control invasive nonnative plants. | H | 2002 | 2017 | 15 | | 12.0 | 180.0 | 0.05/GS 9 0.05/WG 8 | 97707 97704 00702 |
| Conduct prescribed burning. | M | 2004 | 2017 | 13 | 10.0 | 10.0 | 160.0 | 0.05/GS 11 | 00702 |
| Maintain efforts to monitor plover nesting success and band all chicks. | H | 2002 | 2017 | 15 | | 12.8 | 192 | 0.3/GS 5 | n/a |
| Construct and maintain 1,500 feet of wheelchair accessible trail to the river. | M | 2005 | 2007 | 2 | 66.0 | 3.0 | 105.0 | | n/a |

**Table 7. Budget proposal for Salinas River NWR Comprehensive Conservation Plan** *(continued).*

| Project Title | Priority[1] | Start Year | Completion Year | Duration (years) | Operational Cost for Startup (thousands) | Average Annual Cost (thousands) | 15 Year Total Cost (thousands) | Staffing (FTE/ Grade[2]) | RONS[3] |
|---|---|---|---|---|---|---|---|---|---|
| Develop and implement management and monitoring strategies for special status species, including monitoring impacts of public use. | H | 2003 | 2017 | 14 | | 6.4 | 89.6 | 0.05/GS 5 0.05/GS 7 0.05/GS 9 | n/a |
| Inventory and quantify the composition of the grassland on the Refuge. | M | 2002 | 2017 | 15 | 8.6 | 1.0 | 23.6 | 0.1/GS 5 0.1/GS 9 | 97707 97705 |
| Conduct a hydrologic study of the Refuge. | L | 2005 | 2005 | 1 | 75.0 | | 75.0 | | 01702 |
| Complete a two year inventory of the species present in the Salinas River Lagoon. | M | 2007 | 2009 | 2 | 20.0 | 25.0 | 70.0 | 0.2/GS 5 0.3/GS 9 | n/a |
| Develop and maintain GIS database. | M | 2002 | 2017 | 15 | 40.0 | 10.0 | 190.0 | 0.05/GS 11 0.05/GS 9 0.05/GS 5 | 01701 |
| Maintain and enhance partnerships with State Parks to share information and coordinate monitoring. | H | 2002 | 2017 | 15 | | 3.2 | 48.0 | 0.05/GS 11 | n/a |
| Conduct sitewide inventory of potential archaeologic and historic resources and incorporate into interpretive materials. | H | 2003 | 2003 | 1 | 10.0 | | 10.0 | | n/a |
| Annually monitor hunting use of the Refuge. | M | 2004 | 2017 | 13 | | 4.2 | 63.0 | 0.1/GS 7 | 00701 |
| Design and install an orientation kiosk at the Refuge entrance. | M | 2004 | 2005 | 1 | 35.0 | | 35.0 | 0.05/GS 11 0.05/GS 9 0.1/GS 7 | 97702 00701 00702 |
| Improve and maintain the parking lot surface. | H | 2002 | 2017 | 15 | 30.0 | 3.0 | 75.0 | 0.05/WG 8 | 00702 |
| Design and install interpretive signs along trails. | M | 2006 | 2007 | 1 | 32.0 | | 32.0 | 0.05/GS 9 0.05/GS 11 0.1/GS 7 | 97702 00701 00702 |
| Enhance existing environmental education partnerships. | L | 2002 | 2017 | 15.0 | | 2.1 | 31.5 | 0.05/GS 7 | 00701 |
| Develop environmental education and interpretive materials. | L | 2002 | 2017 | 15 | 15.0 | 9.0 | 150.0 | 0.1/GS 7 0.05/GS 11 (EE Supv) | 0.3 |
| Conduct routine maintenance. | H | 2002 | 2017 | 15 | 50.0 | 20.0 | 350.0 | 0.1/WG 8 | n/a |
| Establish a satellite office in the Monterey Bay area as the Refuge expands. | M | 2005 | 2017 | 12 | 120.0 | 40.0 | 600.0 | | n/a |
| Establish and implement program to monitor migratory bird response to riparian restoration. | M | 2002 | 2017 | 15 | 10.0 | 10.0 | 160.0 | 0.1/GS 9 0.1/GS 5 | 97705 |

[1]  Projects are prioritized as high (H), medium (M), or low (L).
[2]  Salary grades are expressed as GS levels 1 15.
[3]  The Refuge Operating Needs System (RONS) is a national database that lists the unfunded operational needs of each refuge. RONS project codes are included in order to update this database with the projects in this CCP.

FTE = full time equivalent (decimal percentage of the hours worked by a full time staff member).

## Step-Down Management Plans

Some projects or types of projects require more in-depth planning than the CCP process is designed to provide; for these projects, the Service prepares step-down management plans. In essence, step-down management plans provide the additional planning details necessary to implement management strategies identified in a CCP. Three step-down plans—the Avian Predator Management Plan, Wildland Fire Management Plan, and Hunting Plan for the Refuge—are included in this CCP as Appendices H, I, and J, respectively.

## Compliance Requirements

This CCP was developed to comply with all Federal laws, executive orders, and legislative acts to the extent possible. Some activities (particularly those that involve revision of an existing step-down management plan, or preparation of a new one) will need to comply with additional laws or regulations besides NEPA and the Improvement Act. In addition to NEPA and the Improvement Act, full implementation of all components of this CCP will require compliance with:

- Executive Order 11988 (Floodplain Management);
- Executive Order 12372 (Intergovernmental Review of Federal Programs);
- Executive Order 11593 (Protection of Historical, Archaeological, and Scientific Properties);
- Executive Order 11990 (Protection of Wetlands);
- Executive Order 12996 (Management and General Public Use of the National Wildlife Refuge System);
- Executive Order 12898 (Environmental Justice in Minority Populations and Low-Income Populations);
- Secretarial Order 3127 (Hazardous Substances Determinations);
- Endangered Species Act of 1973, as amended;
- Refuge Recreation Act, as amended;
- National Historic Preservation Act of 1966, as amended; and
- Coastal Zone Management Act of 1972, as amended.

## Partnership Opportunities

As described in Chapter 1, a number of landowners, State agencies, and educational and scientific organizations conduct research, monitoring, and management activities on or near the Refuge. These partners play an important role in helping the Service achieve its mission and the Refuge's goals. The Service will continue to rely on these and other partners in the future to help implement this CCP and to provide input for future CCP updates. This CCP identifies many projects that provide new opportunities for existing or new partners. There is great potential for more public participation and assistance in the management and interpretation of the Refuge given its proximity to important population centers such as Monterey, Salinas, and Santa Cruz. The Service welcomes and encourages more public participation in the Refuge.

## Adaptive Management

This CCP provides for adaptive management of the Refuge. Adaptive management is a flexible approach to long-term management of biotic resources that is directed by the results of ongoing monitoring activities and new data. Management techniques, objectives, and strategies are regularly evaluated in light of monitoring results, new scientific understanding, and other new information. These periodic evaluations are used over time to adapt both management objectives and techniques to better achieve the Refuge's goals.

Monitoring is an essential component of adaptive management in general, and of this CCP; specific monitoring strategies have been integrated into the goals and objectives described in this CCP whenever possible. All habitat management activities will be monitored to assess whether the desired effect on wildlife and habitat components has been achieved. In order to conduct an effective monitoring program, it is important to establish the baseline, or starting condition. It will also be important to begin studies to monitor the response of wildlife to increased public use of the Refuge in the form of observation and environmental education.

## Plan Amendment and Revision

CCPs are meant to evolve with each individual refuge unit, and the Improvement Act specifically requires that CCPs be formally revised and updated at least every 15 years. The formal revision process will follow the same steps as the CCP creation process (see Figure 3). In the meantime, however, the Service will be reviewing and updating this CCP periodically (at least as often as every 5 years) based on the results of the adaptive management program. This CCP will also be informally reviewed by Refuge staff while preparing annual work plans and updating the Refuge database. It may also be reviewed during routine inspections or programmatic evaluations. Results of any or all of these reviews may indicate a need to modify the plan. The goals described in this CCP will not change until they are re-evaluated as part of the formal CCP revision process. However, the objectives and strategies may be revised to better address changing circumstances or to take advantage of increased knowledge of the resources on the Refuge. If changes are required, the level of public involvement and associated NEPA documentation will be determined by the Refuge Manager.